4037
A Journey in Time

James Barry

Photo -   Eric Sawford

Copyright ©
James Barry 2006

Cover illustration - *Clear Road Ahead* by Terence Cuneo - courtesy of NMSI, London

British Library Cataloguing In Publication Data
A Record of this Publication is available
from the British Library

ISBN 1846852617
978-1-84685-261-9

First Published 2006 by

Exposure Publishing,
an imprint of Diggory Press Ltd,
Three Rivers, Minions, Liskeard, Cornwall, PL14 5LE, UK
WWW.DIGGORYPRESS.COM

Contents

Foreword

IT FELL out of the desk as we moved it. Since that had not been moved since well before my Father died then it must have been there for some years. Clearing my Mother's house we had finally decided to tackle the huge redwood roll-top desk that had held all the family papers and after removing the drawers had tried to move it. After the first lurch towards the door the book hit me on the toe as it fell. It must have been wedged up behind one of the drawers in some discreet void towards the rear. A mottled cloth-covered bound reporter's notebook, with an elastic band around it and grubby edges to the yellowing pages. On the cover in pencil was 'Mar-Aug 1961' in my sparse reportage script – I had never mastered shorthand.

It was a few seconds before I realised what I had in my hand. I was momentarily speared by an image of myself as a much younger man, before marriage, mortgage, children, travelling the world, and much of my life that now stretches behind me. I had been a young aircraft engineer and freelance technical author then, with an idea for a magazine article, and had been told by an Editor to write a piece on the new diesels taking over the railways and how everything would be better and cleaner in the future. Very nice, but even I could see that an era was passing and like sailing ships before them steam locomotives would fade away until one day people asked - 'What happened to them?'

I applied to British Railways for footplate passes through the Public Relations Officer and over a period of time was granted three, one for a diesel hauled express, one for a long distance cross country steam hauled express and one for a branch train. The idea was to sample the old and new of the enginemen's life before steam disappeared forever. In those days we expected steam to be around until about 1975, but as it was it disappeared a lot earlier. In the summer of 1961 diesels were just appearing on the Western Region in significant numbers but the bulk of all traffic was still steam hauled. The following September of 1962 a large cull of 'Castle' class engines took place, and the last 'Castles' ran in everyday service until August 1965. I made the journey as the tide was turning against steam and I experienced the everyday reality of the engineman's lot as it was just before the rundown began - I am glad that I did as it left an indelible impression. I thought then that I should record the scene before it seemingly disappeared forever. I did, and also wrote an article about diesels because that was what they wanted. I had always intended to write the corresponding steam articles from my notes, but other work intruded and then I mislaid the notebook until now - 45 years later.

Engine crews had always been visible but mysterious figures and only three writers have tried to explain the work of men on the footplate to the lay reader - Emile Zola, John Masters and the Reverend A.H. Malan. The steam trips were the more vivid experiences—my legs and arms ached for days afterwards -and reading my notes after over 40 years evoked flashbacks of Technicolor intensity. Its true, you do remember everything you've done, it just takes the right triggers, and this has acted as the impetus for this book. Over the years a fresh perspective takes hold and we can view the recent past from a different standpoint. As I wrote I was constantly amazed at what difficulties these men had to overcome in the nature of their daily work, and moreover how they took it all in their stride.

It's an account not only of a journey, but also an epitaph to a vanished way of life, which while it may now seem quaint or inefficient, worked with a seemingly far higher regard for safety and sound practice than we appear to see today. After the passage of forty-five years the recollection and description of what was then a commonplace really does remind me that 'the past is another country and they do things differently there'. It is an unfortunate fact that the ranks of former steam enginemen are thinning by the year, and first hand knowledge and experience is diminishing. So it falls to me to describe a day in the long life of locomotive 4037, before people say 'Was it really like that. I don't believe it'.... Well, I was there.

James Barry
Co. Wicklow
March 2006

Just to set the scene....

Speeds in 1961 were a great deal 'slower' than now. It's all relative. An express train booked at an average of 60 mph overall was regarded as a fast train. To do that it had to spend much of its time running at 70-80 mph. For the early 1960's this was regarded as very good indeed. Trains running at that speed were usually formed of newer BR-built rolling stock and ran as limited load trains of no more than eight coaches on special timings. An 'average' of 60 mph for a heavier train was regarded as an excellent performance. To average 50 mph over a route with a fourteen coach train was possible but required very great skill by driver and fireman, good coal and an engine in sound condition. Heavier trains were a lot harder to work, in all senses, and could not recover from signal checks or permanent way slacks as quickly as their more lightly loaded brethren. Most relief and extra trains were of the heavy, slower variety, and the speeds quoted in this account, while pedestrian by today's standards were an excellent performance given the load and conditions over that route at the time.

By comparison, and in contrast to today, very few motor cars could be driven safely at over 70 mph, even if they could get up to that speed. The only really fast car on the road then was the newly introduced Jaguar E-type which cost a small fortune by the standards of the day, and there were very few stretches of road in Britain where such a car could be extended in any safety, unless one took it to Germany and sampled the 'Autobahn'. This was Britain just prior to the motorway network, the roads were laid out mainly for cart traffic and the most direct fast routes between urban centres were the railways. It was all so different as to be almost unrecognisable.

For the younger reader, imagine Britain broadly as it is now, EXCEPT - No motorways apart from the M1 and the Preston by-pass, few cars and even fewer foreign cars on the road, no mobile phones, no Internet, no personal computers or laptops, a calculator was a comptometer (what?) or a slide rule (if you knew how to use it), no double-glazing, insulation or central heating in homes, no fitted kitchens (unless you were very well off), no microwave ovens, no McDonalds, very few detached houses (unless very well off), telephones took six months to install and then you would probably have a party line, no jeans or trainers, no fleeces, no Gore-Tex jackets, no beggars, no AIDS, no package holidays, no BBC2 or SKY, only one black and white television in a house and 405 lines at that, no independent or local radio (pirate stations came later) very little domestic refrigeration, very few supermarkets, no drug problem, very few single mothers and living very discretely, no video recorders or DVD's , Pounds, Shillings and Pence, very few air services and all horrendously expensive, V-bombers, Cliff Richard, shorthand typists, stiletto heels, teddy boys, ton-up boys, coal mines, shipbuilding yards, steelworks and foundries, slag heaps and air pollution, The Light Program, Radio Luxembourg, Yuri Gagarin, Kennedy and Kruschev, the Cold War, the Berlin Wall, full employment, Hire Purchase, Purchase Tax and in this pre-Beeching era the quickest way to travel about the country for most people was by train - and we thought, and were told, that 'we had never had it so good'.

June 1961

Chapter 1
Cracking the Flags[1]

BRISTOL TEMPLE MEADS station is Matthew Digby Wyatt's masterpiece. With it's unique overall roof built on a curve sited over a river it was always architecturally ambitious, and more so when you consider that it was built in the 1870's. The station was rebuilt and modernised in the mid-30's to its current form with extra platforms and re-signalled with searchlight colour light signalling. On summer Saturdays like today it's bustling, and the rush will go on all day. It's a hot, dry morning with hardly a cloud in the sky, which is very unusual in our latitudes. A ridge of high pressure had settled itself over the West of England for the previous four days and weather had got progressively drier and now on the fifth day we had a perfect day - it hadn't really cooled down since Friday night - excellent excursion weather. Saturday is change over day in hotels and boarding houses in the West Country resorts, so traffic will be very heavy, and every engine that's fit to run will be at work on extra relief trains and excursion traffic. This goes on during every weekend in the summer season but especially during the last two weeks of July and early August when the Midlands factories, Northern mills and South Wales coal mines are all on 'stop fortnight' and traffic reaches a crescendo as crews, locomotives and stock are stretched to the limit. But it always seems to work, and despite lateness people seem to get there and as Bristol is the major railway crossroads to the West, many long distance holiday trains pass through here and stop for fresh engines or a change of crew.

I did not expect Temple Mead's station to be so busy at nine o'clock in the morning, but it was in the middle of handling a series of overnight holiday trains from the North and industrial

---

[1] When the sun is hot enough over a long period it tends to set up stresses in flagstones which lead to their cracking as dusk falls, hence the term

Midlands to the far West, as well as its normal traffic and nearly every platform was occupied. Wherever I looked there were crowds and activity. Passengers with luggage and children with buckets and spades, barrows piled high with mail waiting for loading, spare and pilot locomotives simmering in bay sidings and on the centre road under the great curved roof, and above it all a huge flock of starlings [2]tracing patterns in the sky like a swarm of bees as they moved in formation around the station.

Like everyone else, I was here in order to leave. I was authorised to travel, so my pass said, on the footplate of a train on the cross-country Bristol to Shrewsbury route. This was for background for an article on 'the changing face of transport' for a technical magazine. I felt that this would be more representative than the usual mad dash to London, so I requested a pass for Bristol - Shrewsbury via Newport, as I knew steam was still used on those services. Seeking out the Station Master, who was a very busy man this morning, but nevertheless welcomed me warmly, I was taken by an assistant to the Inspectors Office at Temple Meads and introduced to Inspector Lewis, my guide and mentor for the day. All official footplate visitors were accompanied, as it allowed the crew to concentrate unhindered, and I could observe and ask questions without distracting them. Inspector Lewis had dealt with journalists before so he knew what I was looking for. I have to sign an indemnity over a two-penny stamp and having checked that I have a valid ticket Bristol - Shrewsbury the paperwork is quickly completed. A pair of RAF overalls, a souvenir of National Service replaces my jacket, and it goes into my holdall with other gear. I also have an old beret, which I will put on later, for use against coal dust. Nobody will take any notice of another man in blue overalls today as there are scores of them around here, this being a major crew changing point.

When I met Inspector Frank Lewis I judged him to be in his early 60's, a heavily built but fit looking man wearing a serviceable dark blue double breasted pin stripe suit, white shirt, a tie and militarily

---

[2] They tried everything over the years, shotguns, dustbin lids, birds of prey and poison, but the starlings still live under the Temple Meads roof.

polished shoes. He sports a trilby hat, as headgear is 'de rigeur' on steam. I never saw an engineman or other footplate occupant without something on their heads. In all other respects he would look like a senior bank manager. However, he is carrying a heavy leather bag of Gladstone style holding an old scarf and dustcoat for footplate use along with other tools of the inspector's trade. An old school GW engineman of pre-First War vintage, a native of Aberbeeg in the Western Valley of Monmouthshire, and a man who had worked Dean Goods engines with Allenby's expeditionary force in Mesopotamia whilst with the Royal Engineers in the First World War. He rejoined the Great Western on demobilisation in 1919 and worked through the ranks firing and driving during the 1920's and 30's at Aberbeeg and Newport where he did a great deal of main line work to all parts of the Great Western, and was promoted to Inspector during the difficult War years, acting as mentor to crews during the blackout and bombing raids. He is a life long steam man, although having made several trips on diesels he appreciates their comfort and predictability but is bothered by their current bouts of unreliability, which is leading to steam substitution on some front rank express services, but as he says with retirement looming he expects steam 'to see him out'.

Making our way through the crowds under the huge roof and along the platform, we walk towards the far end to await our train, joining a small knot of enginemen, engine spotters and a cameraman sitting at the north end of the platform awaiting trains for different reasons. Inspector Lewis is known to several of them and the grapevine is quickly brought up to date. An LMR Jubilee 45682 'Trafalgar' is standing behind us waiting to go to Leeds and a Hall, 4967 'Shirenewton Hall' is easing a ten coach Weston excursion through the centre road. Various pilot engines are moving around adding and detaching vans and coaches from trains. The inspector talks to Control on a nearby phone and is told that our train has passed Uphill Junction 'right time' and has run well from Newton Abbot.

Finishing this conversation, he promises a good run as 'Shrewsbury men are on the job' working home on the return leg of this last lodging turn, which involves a night away from home.

Two depots, Newton Abbot and Shrewsbury share the job, and it's the only lodge turn left on the Western Region as well as having the highest daily mileage. Why do they still do it in the face of Union opposition? Well, 120 miles a day is regarded as a days work with every extra mile paid at enhanced rate so one two-day lodge turn with a combined mileage of about 440 miles allowing for shed to station movements at both ends, plus overnight allowances, leads to a good pay packet at the end of the week. The crews at both depots share the job so everybody gets to dip a spoon in the gravy on a regular basis. Inspector Lewis hinted that several he knew had paid off mortgages early and funded children in University as a result of an association with this particular job, and so it remains, tolerated for its fiscal niceties if nothing else.

The 'Jubilee' gives a whoop on its Stanier hooter and barks away in its steady three cylinder style, hauling its packed Leeds bound train out across the pointwork and onto the relief lines to run up to Filton. The twelve coach train follows, rocking and lurching across the layout, under a cloud of pungent coal smoke from a freshly charged fire. The throbbing three cylinder beat rises and falls as she advances round the curve past Dr.Days Junction and into the cutting at Lawrence Hill, until she's lost to view and peace descends like the coal smoke from her fire.

Our train, running as a Kingswear-Manchester relief slides under the Bath Road Bridge, coasting in under easy steam after its fast sprint across the Somerset levels. Engine 4037 and thirteen coaches, 415 tons tare, about 460 loaded, a near capacity haul for the North & West[3] line for a single 'Castle' class engine and standing room only as far as we can see. It's a variegated train, a mix of liveries, coaches in maroon and cream and plain maroon and in the middle a large twelve-wheeled restaurant car in chocolate and cream. The coaches are Great Western ones of pre-war and post-war vintage and this relief train is obviously made up of second string stock kept for such work.

---

[3] The route from Bristol to Shrewsbury along the Welsh border was always known in GW days and by the Western Region as the North and West line. It was downgraded to a secondary route in the 60's but is still an important artery.

This vast caravan snaked over the crossovers and into the platform road, momentum running out as it came around the curve under the great roof, past many pairs of eyes and 4037 sighed to a gentle stand with an arresting squeal of brakes right at the end, so as to accommodate all of the train in the long curved platform. No fuss, no noise, no steam leaks, just the hot breath from the chimney and an acrid smell of hot metal as 4037 brings it all to a smooth stop – on time. Bedlam begins immediately, mail for Pontypool, Abergavenny, Hereford and points north is thrown into the front van by Royal Mail men in khaki dustcoats while Bristol mail from the west is thrown out. The platform is a seething mass of holidaymakers and more serious travellers' bent on getting seats and luggage in racks for the journey north. Not that I have to worry, I'm to travel in considerable style even if not in comfort.

Our locomotive, 4037 is a veteran built originally in December 1910 as one of the 'Star' class and named 'Queen Philippa', a vision of purposeful Edwardian elegance, designed by a Devonian from Stoke Gabriel who was one of the most brilliant engineer/administrators ever, George Jackson Churchward. She was rebuilt as one of the 'Castle' class in 1926,and renamed as 'The South Wales Borderers' eleven years later in April 1937. Now allocated to Newton Abbot - depot 83A, and a favourite for the 216 mile run to Shrewsbury, which is the longest continuous engine working on the Western Region. She's been comprehensively rebuilt over the last five years and now resembles the proverbial Irishman's gun, the only original parts are probably the brass cabside number plates. New mainframes were fitted in the mid-50's with new cylinders and all running gear optically re-aligned. She was fitted with a repaired boiler from the pool of 'Castle' class spares and trails a newer flat sided high tender of post-war build which reputedly makes firing easier. Since Swindon Works do a thorough repair every time then she is largely a few years old. The paperwork may say otherwise but despite her 'age' she appears in fine condition, and as a result is still booked to first class express work.

She's been freshly steam-cleaned and wiped over with light oil the previous night and apart from insects frying on the smokebox and weather boards, is in well kept condition, not pristine, just well kept. The copper capped chimney shines and is blued with heat into a coloured pattern on the trailing side, and the brass safety valve bonnet and other bright work have been cleaned and oiled over to a smooth mellow gleam. Her mid-green paintwork is lined out with orange and black coachlines and with a tallowed black smokebox and snowy headlamps she, for steam locomotives, like ships are always 'she', looks a well cared for piece of equipment and, as one might admire an elegantly muscular racehorse, a truly thoroughbred express engine.

The newest examples of the 'Castle' class were put into service in 1950, and only now are there plans for their mass replacement by diesels, although some earlier examples from the 1920's have already been withdrawn as they become due for heavy repairs, especially if they have frame or cylinder damage and replacement is deemed necessary. It's not worth undertaking such heavy work on over thirty year old machines so they have been withdrawn a few at a time as their condition dictates, not because they can't do the job - they wouldn't have lasted so long if that was the case. Due to the current bout of diesel unreliability they are still to be found on top class work, but are now being used more on principal cross country and relief trains such as this one. During this summer season, every 'Castle' that's fit to run will be put to work to handle the holiday traffic to and from the West Country and Wales.

(As an aside to modern sensibilities, steam locomotives were always 'she' even those with masculine names. Put this down to the temperament of the machine and it's character, and also the characters that ran them. As Inspector Lewis said with a mischievous chuckle,' they are just like women, if you get it wrong or don't treat them right, they will make your life a misery, so you make sure you do' - which while it may sound strange to today's ears, passed without comment then and may even be a back handed compliment. Ask any married man. As I said, it was a different world.)

The crew are a pair of Shrewsbury men working back home on the return leg of this two-day diagram, and obviously in a hurry to get there. They had had a good steady run up from Newton Abbot and with a clear road had kept time. The climb from Samford Peverell to Whiteball summit had slowed them but they had regained their path as a result of a fast sprint across the levels from Bridgwater. They got a good tenderful of water at Creech troughs and the coal is some good Welsh lump mixed with ovoids[1] and now they know that 4037 is sound are out to get there as quickly as possible. Everything's gone well so far and they are expecting a good trip, so two visitors turning up doesn't appear to cause any disquiet.

Our driver, Fred, is a man in his mid-50's with thick grey hair and a lean fit physique which is kept that way by the odd bout of firing. I was to find that Fred was a great observer with a dry manner, and obviously a man of sharp wit and shrewd intelligence, who happened to be driving express trains, with all of the responsibility that that entails. During the day he, Stan his fireman, and the Inspector imparted sufficient wit, footplate wisdom and job knowledge to astound me even now, as I recount it almost 45 years later. I noted it all at the time as a diligent observer of the scene, little realising what a vivid and contemporary record it was to become. Fred is a grandfather with a wife and two daughters living in Shrewsbury. Both daughters are teachers, of which he is very proud, and as he said, they are off his hands. He only tolerates the double home turn to Newton for its financial compensations as he hopes to 'square everything up in the next few years' and pay off his mortgage.

His mate, Stan, a very fit and alert man in his early 30's, is a passed fireman, which means that he is a fireman who has passed the driver's exam, some six months previously in fact, but goes firing on these jobs between driving turns because of the mileage money and allowances, and because this job demands experienced

---

[1] Known as 'Bronowski's Bullets' these were a briquette in oval form about the size of a man's fist. Wisely avoided due to variable quality they would only be burnt when all else had run out.

old hands. Stan has done enough firing over the years for Fred not to have to worry about hot plentiful steam at the right time in the right place. A married man with two small children he lives outside Pontypool, and is on the Pontypool Road depot paybill, but he has been loaned to Shrewsbury shed for the holiday season as they are short of men, due to Shrewsbury depot's proximity to the West Midlands factories. He gets home on rest days and like Fred says the compensation is the mileage money, especially with small children. He is also being paid his driver's rate and an accommodation allowance as an incentive to help Shrewsbury out so he's happy to do it as long as it does not go on too long. Stan will actually pass his home today but it will be another two days before he will step back over his own front door, but as he says, this arrangement will not last, and it's back to Pontypool Road shed after the holiday rush.

Both men are wearing the blue overall jacket and trousers customary of steam enginemen and the usual headgear as proof against flying soot. Fred has the issue greasetop cap with polished chocolate enamel and brass 'British Railways' badge but Stan has what looks like an old Afrika Korps peaked forage cap, but is in fact a Deutsche Bundesbahn loco fitters cap. He says the leather band on the greasetops irritates his scalp when sweating, so he doesn't bother with them. He had picked this up during a trip to Germany two years ago and has worn it at work ever since. A certain amount of flying dust and dirt is expected in this job, but Fred sports a grey work shirt and tie while his mate has a snowy white PT vest on under his overalls. Considering they had just come seventy-seven miles from Newton on a warm summer morning, they were looking very clean and tidy. Both were wearing polished and cared for work boots with steel toecaps, an absolute necessity when dealing with large lumps of coal in confined spaces. I commented on Stan's use of cycle clips and he tells me it stops coal dust going up your trouser legs. I was to find out the truth of this later in the day.

Two young cleaners from Bath Road shed arrive, carrying firing shovels and Stan beckons them aboard. They climb on top of the coal in the tender and start shovelling and shifting it forward –

this is standard practice at Bristol apparently on summer Saturdays, to try to ease the work of firemen on long distance relief trains like this.

Stan disappears with the tea cans to the refreshment room, and with the Inspector putting his dustcoat on and watching the cleaners, Fred beckons me to follow him as he takes the two-pint feeder from the tray above the firedoor. We climb down, and make our way forward with Fred explaining what he is doing and why, feeling bearings and wheel bosses with the back of his hand for signs of heat, drawing corks and topping up oil boxes, prodding, poking and feeling for slack like a careful doctor examining a patient. He had examined 4037 at Newton Abbot shed, he explains, but the Bristol stop is the first one where he can get down and have another good look, even though he had a quick sniff and prod around at Exeter and Taunton. Steam enginemen always do this he says, and what the eye doesn't see the nose will soon find out about as overheated oil and whitemetal have a distinctive smell. Fred says that if there's going to be trouble he'd rather know about it first, so a quick look round, as circumstances permit is always in order. At the front of the loco, he checks the vacuum pipe for security on its stopper as last week they hit a pheasant at Marshbrook that dislodged the pipe and brought the train to a stand, so it's a second's work to check it and move on. Both lamps are lit and showing a steady light, ready for the Severn Tunnel and passing carefully down the other side he feels crosshead, slidebars and big-ends for heat and runs the back of his hand over wheel bosses. He points out in passing, the different numbers stamped on parts carried by 4037. One connecting rod was formerly on 4075, while the trailing driving wheelset was formerly beneath 5015. 'Star' class 4021 previously carried the other outside connecting rod. The old numbers have had a line stamped through them with 4037 stamped next to them. There are probably other examples on the inside gear. Fred tells me there is nothing underhand about this. He has seen parts on some locomotives, which have been carried by four previous engines. This is one of the benefits of standardisation. When a locomotive is stripped and examined for Intermediate or General Repair it will be reassembled with its old parts or with reconditioned parts from the finished parts stores as a matter of course. It helps to keep repair time down and utilisation high, and is regarded as a sound Swindon practice.

I reach up and run my fingers over the polished regimental crest and nameplate on the splasher. Fred laughs to himself ' I've seen lots of people do that' he says. Both are beautifully hand-finished pieces of work, the nameplate being built up in steel and brass with a dignified serif script and the crest is a heavy bronze casting, a copy of the regimental cap badge several times full size which has been scoured to give a mellow gleam in the sun. They add the finishing touch to an elegant and aesthetically balanced machine.

She's cool and sound all round he says, so we return to the footplate. The two cleaners are just stepping down taking their shovels with them and a mound of coal now shows over the coping at the front of the tender. Stan returns with the teacans and they are put with the oil feeder on the shelf over the firedoor to keep warm. I wondered aloud why they did not take water from the boiler for tea, but Fred looked at me knowingly and said they were only too aware of what was put into it before it reached the tender. Best left alone, he said, unless you felt in need of a drastic laxative.

Fred opens a tender locker and rummaging in his holdall takes out two large West Country pasties wrapped in greaseproof paper which he further wraps in newspaper and puts on top of the condensing coil in the cab roof above his head. There's a space between the coil and the roof which the pasties fit neatly into, and there they'll warm until ready – they'll be right by Abergavenny he says - and they'll probably want them by then. Our guard, an elderly bespectacled man with a braided peaked cap and sporting a buttonhole appears at the cab with a sweating platform inspector. There are so many passengers for the north that an extra coach is being added on Control orders, he says, bringing the load up to 14 which is slightly over the limit for a 'Castle' on this route. Our crew are not entirely happy with this development as it could slow them down, and bang goes any chance of an early finish, but the station pilot is already adding the coach, and they say 4037 is 'a good strong engine with no knocks and blows' which is a rarity these days, so they're willing to try. She has a tenderful of good stuff, Bedwas coal mixed with ovoids, taken from the Newton Abbot stage, which the Bristol cleaners have shifted into the void behind the shovelling plate to replace that burned on the way up. They debate requesting assistance from Bristol with this load and after talking to Control, Inspector Lewis tells them that it'll be at least an hour before either Bath Road or St. Philips Marsh shed can send an assisting engine across. They have a 6800 'Grange' class on the firepit at the moment, but are short of crews. That decides it. Their view is that they'll get home quicker if they do the job themselves rather than hang about for assistance, even if it means crawling over Church Stretton summit at 5 m.p.h. Inspector Lewis confers with the platform inspector and arranges to wire Abergavenny to have a banker available for the climb to Llanvihangel and talks to Control[5] to try to get a guaranteed clear road to Pontypool, as restarting a fourteen coach train even with a good 'Castle' can be problematic depending on where you happen to be stopped, and we don't wish to cause unnecessary delay on a summer Saturday if we don't have to.

She had been well warmed up by her sprint across the levels and pressure is holding steady at 210, with the blower barely on, to keep a haze at the chimney top with no smoke being made while standing. A white hot fire will be required for a fourteen coach load, with careful constant firing to keep pressure up to the mark, at just under 225 lbs. per square inch, which is where it has to be if they are to hold anything like the running times, and keep their path over the road. In fact Stan didn't expect to sit down on the run as he said 'fourteen on' would not allow it on this road, even with a good 'Castle'. He would have to stay right on top of matters if time was not to be lost. 'It'll be a case of slogging up the hills and running very fast down them to keep the overall timings', rather than the steady run they had planned to do. Fred

---

[5] Every division had a control office which handled the running of passenger and freight trains. Signal boxes reported back to them and also carried out their instructions. The running of all trains was closely monitored, as we shall see.

said he hoped I 'wasn't prone to seasickness' in his dry style. I was to find out what he meant later.

Stan has built up what Western men call a 'haycock' fire, with a mound of fresh coal just inside the firedoor, which has the dual purpose of stopping cold air rushing in by warming it on the way, and allowing fresh coal to get properly alight. It also means that there is a quantity of partly burned-through coal handily placed which can be spread about the firebox to build the fire up quickly. The blower[6] is cracked on a further half turn as a few shovelfuls are put in the back corners of the box but the serious work will start once we are under way. Inspector Lewis looks at the mound of coal up over the firehole ring which is burning through nicely and keeping the heat off our trouser legs –'May as well kick that over' he says, so Stan takes the shovel and pushing it down vertically between the rear of the mound and the back wall of the firebox, pulls back and spreads the deep orange coals out further to create a base for more firing later. The back of the firebox is now well covered with bright fresh coal, and this will do for now until she's on the move. Then there's the smell. Steam engines had a unique aroma, a compound of hot oil, sulphur, a tang of bitumen and the acrid stink of hot cast iron, not entirely unpleasant and very distinctive. Once smelt you never forget it.

Stan has a personal rule about only firing onto a hot white fire where possible, so he will wait until she's really working hard before he starts to put large quantities of coal on, so as to cut down on smoke. Smoke denotes incomplete combustion and waste, and never mind an Inspector's presence, Stan is an old enough hand to use his head to save his back. Only the thirteenth shovelfull actually pulls the train he says, so you make sure you get as much out of it as possible. As the overall thermal efficiency of the steam locomotive is about 7-8% this is right, but I have never heard it put that way before.

---

[6] Also known as the 'persuader'. A valve which controlled a jet of steam emitted through a ring at the base of the chimney. This created a strong smokebox vacuum which livened up the fire when standing. Used judiciously due to its steam consumption, it was a necessary evil when pressure had to be kept up to the mark.

The trick of successful firing on these jobs is little and often – chasing the bright spots and putting just the right amount of coal on at the right time. It also means constant movement, as on heavily loaded express work there is plenty for the fireman to do to stay on top of the job. There is an art to firing in the right places- typically the driver thinks three miles ahead but the fireman has to think ten miles ahead or they'll be stuck for steam on the steeper stretches, and with 14 on <u>any</u> gradient has to be regarded as steep. The driver drives with one view of the road in his head, but the fireman fires to quite another with a mental picture of the gradients and signals and the likely effect on steam demand. It is all an exercise in forethought and anticipation, and is not the mere coal shifting job that some people foolishly make it out to be.

Having been silent throughout, 4037 starts to hum to herself, not noisily or nastily, but just like a hive of bees on a summer's day, gently in the background, as if bored and wishing to be on her way. This is characteristic of Great Western safety valves, as they come near to blowing off point - 225 lbs./sq.in - they give an audible warning allowing the deft fireman to put some water in the boiler before wasteful blowing off takes place. Fred and Stan are unconcerned as this is just as they want it. We are about to leave and there is an air of expectation among the relief enginemen and spotters at the platform end to see if we get away cleanly and without fuss with the heavy train. The spotters are waiting for a theatrical display while the enginemen look on with professional appreciation of the task in hand. The searchlight signal flicks to green along with all the other signals along our route setting, over the switches and crossings to the South Wales line. There are shrill whistles and gestures on the platform and it looks like its time to go. In a series of swift movements Stan drops the firehole flap, which has stopped our legs from singeing, shuts the firedoors and fully opens the dampers to his desired setting. Boiler pressure is showing just over 220 on the gauge, and with Inspector Lewis and I moving to the corners of the tender, out of the way, its time as Fred says 'to get the show on the road'.

Chapter 2
Pulling up to Patchway

SITTING on his tip-up seat and looking back over the heads of the crowd, Stan catches the signal from the platform inspector relaying the guard's 'right away' from around the curve, looks across the cab to his mate and says 'Rightaway Fred'. He nods, opens the brake ejector fully to create vacuum in the train, gives an answering whistle, winds her into full forward gear, and with cylinder cocks and regulator opened half-way 4037 eases forward, appears to pause, like a huge dray horse taking the load, and then gently, steadily and with great purpose starts to stride away with the train to the accompaniment of deep throaty barks from the chimney top which echo and resound right across the station. After travelling about fifty yards, Fred shuts the cylinder cocks, the chimney bark rises a full octave and she settles into the load, slipping slightly on the crossings taking us across to the South Wales lines, which Fred quickly checks by shutting and reopening the regulator. The train follows obediently behind, snaking across the points and crossings. Stan looks back for anybody being dragged or any open doors, catching a wave from the guard at the rear, he acknowledges and then looking across the cab to Fred says 'All clear mate' and gives him the nod. The regulator goes up a bit more, towards the cab roof as we pass Bristol box with the signalmen looking down from the operating floor. We're passing the Midland line junction at Barton Hill and start to ease across onto the South Wales lines as we curve around to the junction signalbox at Dr.Days Bridge. All signals are clear, and the signalman and booking boy are watching us leaving with this huge train and urging us on with waves and big grins. 4037 must look a fine sight, brass and copper shining, clean green paintwork and a clear stack giving off a tremendous accompaniment as we get the train out of Bristol Temple Meads as fast as we decently can. Watching the pair at Dr.Days giving us the once over, it comes home to me how much scrutiny of passing trains takes place. This is drummed into railwaymen of all grades - not only must they stand clear when trains are passing but keep a sharp look out for anything untoward. We will be watched and examined by many knowledgeable observers on the way North, signalmen, other enginemen on passing trains, shunting engine crews and permanent way gangers – passengers are often unaware of this.

As manpower has declined so the scrutiny of passing trains has declined and safety must suffer. Experienced railwaymen knew what to look for and had a shrewd capacity for nipping potential trouble in the bud before it became a serious problem. This was the cornerstone of safety and was taken very seriously. If a signalman or any other watcher suspected anything amiss then action was taken and a 'Stop and Examine' instruction sent to arrest the train at the next signal box. It is no coincidence that the old Great Western went for almost forty years without a single passenger fatality, due to the sound methods of observation and operational care drummed into the staff at all levels. That fine record was only ended due to a tragic accident to a sleeper train at Norton Fitzwarren during the Second World War.

Passing the box, Stan gets up and opens the firedoors to reveal an angry bright orange fire dancing to the exhaust's beat, and taking the shovel proceeds to have a look. By holding the tip of the shovel just inside the firehole, turning it upside down and angling the airstream under it to point to a desired part of the firebox, he can look along the line of the shovel and see if any holes have been pulled in the firebed by the blast up the stack and the movement of the engine. She looks set for now, and so he pulls up the firehole flap plate to leave a small quadrant of the firehole open for secondary air and turns to the tender. Sliding the shovel under the coal, he takes the coal pick and turns a large lump of coal and hits it twice along the grain. It splits neatly into lumps just over the size of a man's fist, which is about the right size for what he has in mind. He then turns and sets the exhaust steam injector to his liking.

This clever device has no moving parts and has a side effect of heating the water as it feeds it to the boiler using exhaust steam that was going up the stack anyway. It's a cunningly economical device and an indispensable tool for express running the Inspector tells me. Now that the regulator is well open there is enough exhaust pressure for it to operate cleanly, and so he sets it to maintain a steady boiler water level and looks out for the Lawrence Hill signals, giving the nod to Fred for those he can't readily see and looks back along the train stretched out around the curve. There are windows open and heads at carriage doors all along the train on this hot morning, and as its starting to cool a little on the footplate it must be cooling down now on what would have been a hot muggy train whilst standing under the roof at Bristol.

We're passing along a large retaining wall on the fireman's side and the Inspector crosses the cab and listens for the sound of any looseness and knocks, being reflected off it. Apart from a slight ringing of the rods, she's sound and he looks well satisfied.

I question the background ticking, in time with every revolution of the wheels. This is the vacuum pump, driven off the valve gear between the frames. It's there to overcome any leakage of vacuum in the train brakes and try and ensure the brakes don't 'leak' on or drag. Other railways do this by use of a small steam vacuum ejector[7] instead of the large one, but the Western always use a pump. The Western brakes run at 25 inches of vacuum rather than the BR standard of 21 inches. On passenger trains the leakage may not be that great as with fourteen coaches on there are only seventeen flexible hose joints to worry about, including three on the engine and tender. On fully vacuum fitted freight trains it will be a lot more than that and one or two joints drawing air would slow the train if not bring it to a stand. The pump is there to take care of this, as a continuously running small ejector would be a considerable drain on steam and water. The ticking of the pump was also a useful way to estimate speed in the days

---

[7] Passing steam through several cones in a closed chamber produces a vacuum. Another device with no moving parts that was used to create vacuum throughout the braking system, hence vacuum brakes. Air brakes work the opposite way round (if that makes sense!)

before speedometers were fitted, and drivers became quite adept at it. Stan tells me he's glad its summertime and we don't have to heat the train as well as this would consume even more coal and water than they intend to get through.

Fred opens the regulator wide and sets the reverser to 30%. At this, 4037 starts to steadily accelerate through the suburban station of Lawrence Hill and really gets hold of the train, the exhaust from the stack sounding like machine gun fire. We've got the whole train away from pointwork and on to the straight, speed is rising as the exhaust resonates off the lineside houses and passing a small playground on the left hand side all games are suddenly stilled as the children watch us go by with a whistle and a wave from the cab.

Stan drops the flap to reveal a seething nearly white fire, and taking the shovel, loads its tip with some of the freshly broken lumps and neatly sends them through the door, angling the shovel as he does so to put each charge just where he wants it. At no time does he move his feet, its all done from one position using the length of the shovel and the swing of his body to impart speed and movement to the coal to project it neatly onto the firebed in just the right place. The jolting and jarring as 4037 runs through pointwork and over rail joints does not bother him as he's standing loosely braced against the movement and using the loaded shovel as a counterweight. It looks backbreaking work, but Stan says you get used to it, and you certainly won't get middle-aged spread. It explains succinctly why he looks so fit, the heat of the footplate together with the continuous movement means that fat gets sweated and worked off before it has time to stick. His economy of movement is superb, there's nothing wasted and he has placed himself so that everything he needs to attend to can be reached with the least amount of effort. (Twenty five years on, he could have made a nice living as an aerobics instructor, but work for leisure was in nobody's mind in those days)

They've worked her up to 50 by now, and the distant and home signals for Stapleton Road are all off and with a screech on the

whistle, warning bystanders on the platform to stand back, we
thunder through, over the bridge at the far side and onto the
Filton incline that rises away in front of us in very noticeable
fashion. I had never seen it from the cab before, and by the end of
the day there was much I observed from the cab that was a world
of difference away from the view from the train. The adjacent
goods yard sidings fall rapidly away from main line showing how
steep the gradient quickly becomes, 1in 75 all the way to Filton.
Across an embankment looking back towards Bristol basking in
the sunshine and running over Narrowways Hill Junction where
the line to Clifton Down and Avonmouth goes off to the left, we
continue curving and climbing up past the stern Victorian façade
of the Muller Orphanage that looks down on Ashley Hill station.
She's really got the train by the tail now, even on the long curve,
and urging it on over the bridge by a small coalyard where a
pannier tank is playing with a few wagons, we pass on over the
sand drags, put in to stop runaways down the incline, and onto the
steepest part of the climb. 4037 is well into the task, bringing the
14 well filled coaches up the bank at a steady 32mph - very good
going after the flying start, the fire has really woken up and is
making steam, she's holding a steady pressure at 223 with just a
purl from the safety valve and showing two thirds of a glass of
water. Inspector Lewis looks on approvingly, this is as about as
good as it can be, given our load. Stan is deftly putting small
amounts of coal just where he wants it, tickling her palate with
tasty morsels and keeping her white hot all over the box.

There's a housing estate on the right hand side and a bunch of
boys with notebooks standing at the fence watching us as we
hammer by, some of them looking back and counting the
carriages, others looking at the light grey exhaust being shot up
high into the clear sky by each whipcrack exhaust beat. Stan is
steadily feeding her small shovelfulls now, to different parts of the
firebox, and after each one the exhaust goes slightly grey and then
clears again. Looking behind you can see distinct clouds of light
grey in our wake. He pulls the flap plate up and then drops three
shovelfuls over it leaving it in place with just a quarter of
the firehole showing. This gives her enough air for efficient

combustion without being too much which may cool her down. The fire is white hot, the flap is being banged against the firehole by the suction of each exhaust beat, and the note of the exhaust is sharper as the train is stretched straight out below Horfield, a suburban station on the gradient and set in a cutting. She's down to 27mph now, still pulling well but feeling the weight of the small town hung on behind her.

Just past Horfield the gradient eases and we come to the top of the incline where the track levels out. This seems very pronounced as seen from the cab, the 14 coaches are hanging heavy but the white hot fire is holding pressure steady at 210 with a wide open regulator and cutoff now wound out to 40%. There's a sharp steady purposeful bark from the stack, no steam leaks, all beats evenly spaced with nothing out of tune, denoting a clean front end in excellent shape, the Inspector judges her to be in good condition all round and well equal to the task. If we can manage Filton incline like that, then we should be able to manage the others, is the way he sees it. Now that we've reached the top in brisk style, he knows what sort of machine he is dealing with. At Filton Junction the South Wales line curves round through the station and onto the straight past the end of Filton airfield – the home of both the Bristol Aeroplane Company and Rolls-Royce aero engines. The signals for South Wales are clear and as all of the train climbs onto level track speed rises as we diverge onto the straight through the station. Now that she's good and hot Fred opens her up to find her pace and adjusts the sight feed lubricator by his left leg to give slightly more oil. The water in the glass has dropped to half, since we came off the hill, but the exhaust injector is singing away and holding the level as 4037 gathers speed along the straight towards Patchway. Stan puts eight quick shovelfulls onto the white fire and as we start to purr along the straight a Bristol Britannia roars in low over our head to land on the Filton runway, startling us as we had not noticed it over our own din. Further, far above but below the high cloudbase I glimpse the vapour trails of a westbound jet aircraft, which is gleaming in the sun. These are usually the objects of my attentions, but today I am getting more closely acquainted with another generation of fast travel a lot closer to earth.

Patchway distant is off and the Patchway signalman is standing at his window watching as we run through the station and head off downgrade towards Patchway Tunnel. On the subject of signals, they run in the sequence, distant, home, inner home and starter, as one approaches the box from either direction. The distant gives advance warning of the setting of the others. If a distant signal is set to Danger, with its arm horizontal, you can pass it at caution but be prepared to stop at any of the others if they are set at danger. The distant signal has a yellow arm with a black stripe to show it is a distant, and shows an amber or green light at night. The others have red arms with a white stripe and show either red or green at night. These were semaphore signals, used since the earliest days of railways, and the arm in the horizontal position meant 'Stop', while when pointing downwards at over 45 degrees it meant 'all clear'. It is a very simple and unambiguous system. Any signal with a red arm at danger along your line means 'Stop', even if you have just passed a distant signal showing clear. All crews knew the positioning of every signal along the route, and look out for them, especially those that are hard to see. The signals are weighted so that in the event of failure or mishap they 'fail-safe', so a snapped signal wire would return the signals to danger. Even if a crew has passed a distant signal at clear they still keep a sharp look out for all the other signals in the sequence. Nothing is taken for granted and passing a signal at danger, even inadvertently is both an enquiry and disciplinary matter, and is always investigated. It is another aspect of the job of which the public is unaware, but forcefully demonstrated when travelling up front.

Chapter 3
Under the English Stones

THE downgrade starts at the platform end and the track drops sharply towards Patchway tunnel entrance along the upper level of a split-level embankment. We are on the down South Wales line while the up South Wales line is at a lower level and lesser gradient. Both lines pass through single line bores of the Patchway tunnels but the one we are entering is on a somewhat steeper gradient to its neighbour. We sweep past the curious split level signalbox by the A38 bridge plummeting on towards the tunnel down the 1 in 80, speed has risen to 55 on the down grade and seen from the cab the tunnel mouth looks frighteningly small. There's a very large plaque on the wall commemorating its opening as part of the 'Bristol and South Wales Union Railway' but before I can read it, with a shrill whistle, we dive into the blackness. Stan had shut the firedoors and put the blower on as it's a narrow bore and we don't want a blowback even though she's working hard and making plenty of draught. 4037 is riding steadily and well and running before the train with everything stretched taut. The sudden draught as we enter the tunnel causes coal dust and other small debris to billow upwards from the floor, and the magnified noise of the locomotive and train allied with the vibration and lurching and the rush of cold air in the tunnel from the heat outside is a real shock to the senses. The noise from the engine and the jointed track, as well as a magnified crunching noise from the ballast below are unnerving to the novice and cause some alarm. There's nowhere for it to go in the narrow bore and I am concentrating on hanging on with gritted teeth. The crew are totally unperturbed by this. They were ready for Patchway tunnel and I was not. The people in the train will find it pleasantly cooling after the heat outside – I just hope they remembered to shut the windows. We flash out into the sunshine doing 70 and then into a shorter bore and pass out into a cutting running alongside the up line which is on a lesser grade. There's a small signalbox, Cattybrook Siding, controlling a crossover and access to a brickworks at Cattybrook, and a long length of straight leading to the station at Pilning. As we career downhill with speed rising into the low 80's, across the fields we can see the Severn and the hills of Wales in the sunshine under a clear summer sky. That's a rarity seeing how much it usually rains and Stan comments to the Inspector on the spell of good weather. A Cardiff based 'King', 6023 hiding behind a huge reporting number on it's smokebox, roars past on the up line at a slightly higher level with a train of chocolate and cream stock heading for London, as we rush pell mell to Pilning, on to the short level stretch, whistling through the station under clear signals we hit the start of the down grade to the Severn Tunnel, passing a long van train in the goods loop at Ableton Lane behind a BR Standard 9F waiting for the road to Wales. Stan puts eight shovelfuls round the box while she's pulling hard down the grade and with the doors shut, blower on and travelling at the full 75 limit we whistle long and loud and plunge into the Severn Tunnel.

The Severn Tunnel bore is larger than Patchway's and double tracked so the dust isn't raised as much. It's a little smokier as trains pass through frequently with engines working hard against the grade. The gradient is 1 in 90 down for about two miles, then level for a few hundred yards, then 1 in 100 up for two further miles with ninety degree bend towards the end to bring it out parallel with the main line on the South Wales side of the river. At the lowest point, under The Shoots, we are about fifty feet below the riverbed before starting the climb up and out.

4037 is rocking and rolling gently in the darkness and the noise is terrific from the engine and train, being reflected and magnified by the tunnel walls. The lurid light from the fire shows us all in stark relief and the air in the tunnel is actually quite cold and damp after the warmth outside. The only other light is from a small gauge-glass oil lamp which illuminates the level in the single boiler water gauge. There is no electric lighting in the cab. Fred's giving her enough steam to keep her taut against the train so she's not bucking and bouncing but riding well as the track in the Tunnel is kept in exemplary order. The Inspector tells me there's a special Tunnel gang that just looks after the track in here. I've spotted a lamp or two in lineside refuges set back into the walls so there's definitely somebody down there. They have pumps running constantly at Sudbrook to deal with the water seepage that runs into a drainage heading below the main tunnel and he tells me that if they were to stop the tunnel would be flooded to the roof at the bottom, in about twenty minutes. They pump millions of gallons of water a day out of the tunnel to stop this from happening, and the pumps run 24 hours a day, 365 days a year. The water is pure and comes from the Big Spring, which caused problems during construction. They've been trying to find its source for years, with dyes and boreholes, either in the Forest of Dean or the Cotswolds but to no avail. The water doesn't go to waste, there's a paper mill at Sudbrook next to the pumping station and a pipeline has been laid to the new Llanwern Steelworks to supply water for steelmaking, so the pumping operation probably pays for itself.

This is every ride you've ever had on the fairground Ghost Train, magnified at least ten times, and just as I was getting used to it and holding on for dear life, with a whistle, roar, flashes of firelight and cloud of smoke and steam a double-headed freight passes in the opposite direction, adding to the fright, din and confusion. Once the smoke has cleared Stan is looking forward out of the cabglass. He and Fred see it at the same time, the marker lights for the bottom of the Tunnel. We're under the English Stones. Although still travelling at just over 70 Fred opens her right up and the noise becomes almost intolerable. We're on the flat at the bottom with the weight of the train behind us, and this should give added momentum. She's really hammering away as she hits the bottom of the 1 in 100 to climb up from below the Severn, beneath the Welsh Stones to daylight two miles ahead.

At this point we cannot see anything, we are in total darkness apart from the gauge glass lamp and the brilliant firelight seen through the small air hole left between the two closed firedoors and may as well be travelling in space. There are low wattage bulbs in the lineside refuges about every hundred yards but that is about it. It is tremendously noisy, frightening and eerie to the newcomer but the other three take it in their stride. Stan opens the doors wide and starts to put small shovelfulls in at intervals around the box, the white fire illuminating us, the tender, the dripping tunnel walls and the front of the train in almost stroboscopic fashion as it pulses to the exhausts urgent beat. With the change in grade she's showing three quarters of a glass of water and holding pressure at 220. Stan shuts off the exhaust injector that has been on since Lawrence Hill and she gains a few pounds in pressure. Fred gives her a quarter turn more on the screw and pushes the regulator right up to the stop, as she now must have the whole train on the upgrade and as the air clears her rapid gunshot exhausts are bouncing off the roof just over our heads. The atmosphere is getting a bit thick as we round the ninety degree bend still travelling at a respectable 55 and in the distance we can see daylight, which is becoming steadily bigger as we forge towards it. The noise, smoke, steam, smell of brimstone, vibration and sensation of power in the confined space is almost overwhelming, I'm sweating and cold at the same time, with the searing heat of the fire on one side and the clammy wetness of the tunnel on the other and a good deal of shock and fright between. Fred and Stan are on their respective sides, looking ahead and the Inspector is standing on the fall plate between engine and tender with one hand on the cab handrail to steady himself watching water level and pressure gauge which are both looking healthy. Nearing the exit 4037 starts to blow off, steam billowing back into the cab and being drawn towards the open firehole and as we finally explode into the sunshine Stan moves quickly to put the exhaust injector back on to shut her up. She's down to 45 as we pass Severn Tunnel West box with the exhaust echoing back off the rock cutting, and the signals are showing clear as we come up the grade to enter Severn Tunnel Junction. There's a man standing in the cess[8] at the bottom of the cutting next to our running line, some three hundred yards ahead. He acknowledges our warning whistle and stands well clear. His hands appear to be full, and as we pass the Inspector shouts a greeting and the man

---

[8] The cess is the walkway either side of the track, where there are usually drainage ditches. The 'four foot way' is the track itself and the 'six foot way' is the distance between the tracks on double and multiple lines.

breaks into a big grin and waves a ferret at us. He's got a ferret in the other hand and there are a few wooden boxes at his feet. The ferrets look unperturbed, as if this happens every day of the week. On reflection, it probably does. The 'Severn Tunnel Ferret Man', I'm told. All the crews look out for him and he's a well-known character. The problem is one of rabbit warrens undermining embankments, which can cause track slippage. This is a huge headache for the Civil Engineers given the tall embankments carrying track either side of the Tunnel. The answer is the ferret man, whose friends clear the warrens so that they can be pumped full of concrete grout and the embankments stabilised. The rabbits are shared out amongst the platelayers. During rationing, this man and his friends fed most of the nearby village of Undy by themselves, so I'm told. Whether this is a tall story or not I don't know, but from my memories of the black market of those days I wouldn't discount it.

Chapter 4
Croeso I Gymru

SEVERN TUNNEL JUNCTION is the gateway to Wales and has a large busy loco depot that supplies engines for tunnel assistance and shunting in the marshalling yards that surround the station. We pass the depot, full of engines on the right hand side and run over the junction and through the station at a steady 50, whistling to warn passengers to stand clear, with the train pouring through the junction behind us. To left and right are freight trains with assisting Tunnel engines attached and on the hump behind the platforms a '9400' class pannier is pushing a long train of vans over it for splitting and marshalling. Looking back in the sunshine, heads are starting to appear at carriage windows again after the tunnel and they must all be nicely cooled down by now as the train is dripping wet from end to end. She's still at full regulator and Fred has wound her back to 35% leaving her roaring lustily from the stack. Across the fields we can see the Severn and Portishead on the opposite bank in the sunshine. Fred stands back for a moment to light his pipe, which has been in his hand for some time. Stan is busy putting coal in the right places, so motioning me to take his place he takes mine at the water scoop handle and as we pass the end of the yard at Undy Ground Frame, down goes the scoop for a fill from Undy troughs. The gauge showing 2500 gallons starts to rise quickly as we pass down the troughs and just short of 4000 Fred deftly winds it back up and secures it with a chain. Turning back across the bucking footplate he guides me back to my place and resumes his place at the regulator. Taking a long puff on his pipe and blowing a stream of smoke my way he asks laughingly 'Seasick yet...you didn't look too happy in the Tunnel?'.... and I suppose I didn't. 'Don't worry ' he says laughing,' most people have never seen or heard anything like it in their life, but they all want to come back and go through again'. He had a point. It was like a ride on the roller coaster through Hell, and if you could sell high-speed trips on the footplate through the Severn Tunnel you would probably make a lot of money.

'That's the last downhill we'll see for a bit – it's fairly flat but for a few lumps and bumps to Newport then all collar work to Pontypool'. As we come round the bend from the troughs we begin to overhaul an iron ore train running on the relief lines made up of roller-bearing fitted box wagons, bauxite in colour with the words IRON ORE TIPPLER painted on them. It's moving quite fast, at about 50, and the guard is standing on the veranda of his van looking down the train. It is taking a while to pass this train as we are only doing about 55 at this point, and at the head is 92250, the Giesl fitted 9F 2-10-0 which is rasping away with this train down the relief road of this four track main line. The Inspector tells me this is an ironstone ore train from Banbury to Cardiff East Moors, which is a prestige freight working and with all the wagons having roller bearings and continuous vacuum brake it'll continue at pretty well this pace all the way to Cardiff. The fireman is hard at work as we pass the cab, and the driver gives us a nod as we pass him. The Inspector gives him the thumbs-up having scrutinised the train of tipplers as we passed it, so the driver will be reassured that nothing is hanging or dragging on his blind side.

It is reasonably flat to Newport, as the line runs across coastal levels, first round the curve to the right to run through Undy Halt then down the four track main line through Magor, where a cement train headed by 4150 was being discharged into a large hopper in the goods yard. 4037 has settled down to a healthy steady roar and is riding like a first-class saloon, with every rail joint being just barely felt. She really is in very good order and the Inspector tells me that she must have recently been in the shops for weighing or spring adjustment as it feels like she has reconditioned back end springs down below. Locomotive springs are massive leaf plate affairs, under the axleboxes that can be adjusted and changed at regular intervals. The only problem with the leaf springs is breakage or loss of camber in the spring plates due to the immense hammering they receive under normal conditions of service, and the rear loco set get the worst hammering of all. A complete set of springs nearing or needing renewal would be giving us a very heavy and harsh ride with the loco rolling into every bad joint and soft spot in the track. A good set allows us to almost float along as the spring gear absorbs all of the irregularities that occur in even well maintained track. We're on straight track and pulling hard, so 4037 is sitting down on her rear springs, but they are still doing a very good job of shock absorption, and a steady drumming vibration through the cab floorboards is all that can be felt. The Inspector tells me that the gentle side to side swaying is to be expected, and is not at all dangerous. The dangerous type of swaying and 'hunting' is a lot sharper and more pronounced than this and is as a result of wheel tyre and flange wear as well as springs that need changing. A locomotive in this condition would be booked to semi-fast or stopping trains until a visit to shops could be arranged. With what he has seen on the climb to Filton and the fast descent to the bottom of the Severn, he has no qualms about 4037's fitness for express work and is anticipating a good steady run all the way to Shrewsbury.

Speed had risen to 70 once again as we passed the flyover at Bishton Crossing and onto the long straight past the new steelworks at Llanwern. This has been four years in the building and is due to open next year. It is three and a half miles long and has a vast internal rail system. Coming down the straight very fast toward us is a brightly polished 'Castle' class engine - 5013 'Abergavenny Castle' - sporting polished brass and burnished copper and silver buffers. She's a Swansea Landore engine and the silver buffers and shipshape order are a Landore trademark, and on a day like this a sight to behold. There's a polished brass oilbox on her inside cylinder casing, which is flashing and reflecting the sunlight like a crown jewel. The closing speed of them and us is in the region of 150 mph and she's scorching along, it seems, with about twelve coaches in tow. With a shriek on the whistle she slams by and the wake and turbulence of her passing raises a fair amount of coal dust off our cab floor. Now I see why the handbrush and slacking pipe are always in use. The dust gets everywhere, as I found later.

We're approaching the outskirts of Newport now, passing Llanwern station on the long straight. The next landmark is Lliswerry Crossing with its wartime signal box and a long queue of traffic on either side of the crossing. There's so much rail traffic on this line that operating a level crossing here must be a very intense business. In the distance Fred can see the distant signal for Maindee set at caution and so winds the reverser into the drift setting and eases the regulator. His hand is on the brake handle but does not move it. As we near the signal the ATC [9]siren near his head goes off, as a warning that we are passing a distant signal at caution, and Fred takes a few inches of vacuum out of the brake to check the train. Coming round the curve at East Usk and onto the straight we can see the home signals for Maindee set at danger about a mile ahead. Opening the vacuum ejector he applies the brake gently and the simultaneous creation and destruction of vacuum in the system allows the deceleration of the train to be carefully controlled as he intends to creep up on the signal like a cat approaching a mouse. Fred doesn't want to kill the momentum if possible, as the restart is followed by a sharp check-railed curve round to the Hereford line and a fourteen coach train is very sticky at low speed on a curve like that so there will be stack music right across town as we get away. Speed is dropping away and heads are starting to appear at carriage windows, looking out to see the reason for the deceleration. After the climb out of the tunnel and the fast run along the marshes, a funeral creep through the suburbs of Newport is hardly exhilarating. In the distance, the reason for the check, 6999 'Capel Dewi Hall' all shone up by Cardiff Canton depot for an inter-regional service, crosses the junction with a train of green Southern Region stock bound for Portsmouth. She hammers by on the up main and passes us in fine style accelerating her train quickly away from Newport. We are still moving ahead at about 3 mph – the speed of a strolling man – when the signal clears and we get the road for the Hereford line. The regulator goes up against the stop and 4037 starts barking

_____

[9] Automatic Train Control - a device introduced by the Great Western in 1906 to stop a train if it passed a distant signal at caution. A siren goes off if this happens, a bell rings if all clear. Both have to be cancelled by the driver or the brakes go on. It cannot be ignored.

long and loud. Stan pulls the firehole flap up and sits down with a well-earned cup of tea. Across the junction we go and hit the curve at 10 mph with the exhaust snapping out like shotgun blasts. Looking back along the train there are heads at nearly every window to see what the noise is all about. The train is squealing against the check rails so Fred gives her 50% cut-off to put a spring in her step, and overcome the extra friction. Crossing the bridge over Caerleon Road bystanders and pedestrians are looking up to see where the noise is coming from and as we go over the safety valve begins to lift. Fred gives her a bit more on the screw and we drag the cavalcade around the curve and across Maindee North junction onto the Hereford line. We must look a fine sight from the train and many are at windows and droplights looking out to see and hear the engine working hard at low speed, and on such a sparkling summer morning.

Maindee North's outer signals are off and as the train is clearing the junction Fred leaves the regulator where it is and drops her to 40% maintaining her punch and pace and bringing the train up to a reasonable speed. We pass a freight behind an ash grey 6300 standing in a refuge loop at Maindee North, waiting for us to pass and once he's got the train up to 45 with a tremendous noise from the stack, Fred shuts off, and lets 4037 and its train coast, freewheeling on but gradually losing speed. There's a permanent 30 over the River Usk bridge at St. Julians and just as calculated we roll gently onto the bridge at exactly 30 and rumble over. Once off the bridge and onto a super elevated curve Fred opens her right up again for the climb up to Caerleon along what the crew wryly call 'Murder Mile' due to the high number of fatalities here. There is a large psychiatric hospital nearby and a sharp lookout is kept for anybody near the track. This is one of the aspects of footplate work no one is anxious to discuss as railwaymen hate fatalities on the job, but it is a reality and there are several black spots on this line where watch is habitually kept. The mess room grapevine keeps everyone's knowledge up to date and nothing appears in official notices, but a few words from the Inspector is all that it takes.

Fred and the Inspector keep a good look out as 4037 accelerates the long train off the curve and up the grade to Caerleon. Stan is busy. Now she's opened up he will be shovelling all the way to Pontypool to get a good fire into her for the climb to Llanvihangel which is a good twenty miles away. He's working methodically to a steady pattern born of long experience, building up a solid seething tapering fire to just the right depth and consistency. He's firing onto a snowy white mass and the exhaust is staying clear which is a sign that she's good and hot. The water level is holding steady at about half a glass, and once through Caerleon and around the long curve Fred will ease her on the reverser to let the injector bring the glass back up to just over two-thirds. The pressure gauge is rock steady at just under 225 and a feather of steam is showing from the safety valves. Caerleon signals are all at clear and the signalman viewing us from behind some young tomato plants[10] gives us the 'all clear' as we run through the curved platforms of this country station past the small goods yard and a '6400' tank and autocoach unloading passengers. They've worked her up to 60 now and the stacatto exhaust is making a fine noise. We round the long left hand curve with 4037 nosing gently from side to side in time with the piston thrusts and chattering healthily from the chimney top and there's a Collett 2200 class shunting the Star Brickworks siding at Ponthir, and as we pass under a road bridge, and looking across farmland I see a vixen and fox cubs crossing a field near where it slopes up beside the line. She looks at the fiery monster with a mild interest, intent no doubt on other things, the cubs trots obediently behind. I point this out to the Inspector and he says that you see much of nature from the footplate. Animals accept steam engines as just another great noisy animal that won't hurt them; it's people they are wary of.

On the bend just below Ponthir station there's a train coming toward us on the down line. An eleven coach rake of ex-LMS stock behind a Western Region 'County' class 1020 'County of

---

[10] Several of the signal boxes we passed had small potted vegetation or plants inside the windows. Due to the glass it gets quite warm in signal boxes, the ideal place for forcing on small young tomato plants. A little perk of the job that some signalmen enjoyed.

Monmouth'. With a warning shriek she rushes by southwards, running under easy steam towards Caerleon. The Inspector tells me the 'thousands' are well respected for their hill climbing abilities on this route, and are able to accelerate away from permanent way slacks and station stops with tremendous verve. They are two cylinder engines as against our four cylinders, but have a smaller driving wheel at six foot three rather than our six foot eight and a half, and in hill climbing a smaller wheel is a great advantage. He says its down to their higher boiler pressure of 250 lbs. per square inch and the fact that they have Stephenson valve gear rather than our Walschaert gear which gives an advantage on the hill sections due to the characteristics of the gear and the way Swindon set it.

The old '2900' or 'Saint' class were great hill climbers on this route and they had six foot eight drivers, two cylinders and the Stephenson gear and were well respected by the crews. The 'thousands' were built just after the war to allow the last 'Saints', which were worn out, to be withdrawn, but in our crew's opinion a good 'thousand' cannot hold a candle to a 'good' Saint, and are less comfortable to ride on due to a teeth rattling fore-and-aft vibration at certain settings of the valve gear. Given that the '1000's' have a power classification just below a 'Castle' and the '29's' were somewhat less this seems strange, but our crew and the Inspector are adamant. 'Can't beat a 29 for hill climbing, the only thing we have to touch it are the 6800 class', which are the small-drivered 4-6-0's, the same size as a 'Hall' but with smaller wheels. In their opinion a 'Saint' is preferable to a '68' which is preferable to a '1000' over this road, and it's definitely horses for courses as 'Castles' 'are fine for flatland work but have to be hit hard to get up the hills. A 'Saint' or '68' wouldn't be so laboured on the banks, and a '1000' would do a good job due to its brute strength, as long as it was climbing. When its coasting, take your false teeth out and put them in your pocket'.

This surprised me as 4037 seemed to be doing a very able job, but in their opinion the 29's or 68's would attack the grades like a terrier. Even though the '29's' were a 'high wheeled engine' the setting of the Stephenson gear and their steam raising capacity gave them the edge. They've been gone eight years now, and that leaves the favourite as the '68' class, which they tell me has five foot eight wheels and specially designed cylinders with a large steam chest capacity, which in their opinion make it a small wheeled '29'. But, they tell me not to worry, 4037 will get us there just the same, she will just have to be 'hit harder to do the same job. The valve gear on these is all right for the flat, but not for steeplechases', as Fred put it, and since they do this every working day I am prepared to take their word for it.

We're climbing up the shallow valley of the Afon Llwyd on a ruling grade of 1 in 90 more or less, away from the Usk valley and towards the rampart of hills that is the beginning of the Welsh valleys. Its pastoral countryside from the east to this point and then the huge twelve hundred foot mass of Twm Barlwm and Mynydd Maen shows up running all the way from Newport to Pontypool. We will skirt this line of hills all the way up the Welsh border and they were a great natural defence in previous years and one reason why the Welsh language never died out. Above the small station at Ponthir still steadily climbing we hit a long lazy S-bend on the 1 in 100 grade. Normally a good 'Castle' with ten coaches would sail up here in fine style says Stan, as he knows this stretch very well, but with fourteen coaches he's got to give her plenty to chew on to keep her going at a steady speed. She's accelerating slightly in spite of everything, and passing Llantarnam Abbey through the trees we pass under a road bridge and thud steadily away through Llantarnam station redolent of a heavy sweet smell of baking biscuits from the Weston's factory next door. The smell is well worth the lungful and makes a change from the charge of sulphur we got at the bottom of the Severn. The goods yard is full of wagons being loaded with biscuits and 1504, one of the rare 1500 class tanks is shunting the cold store on the left hand side as we pass the box at Llantarnam Junction. Its here that the Eastern Valley line to Cwmbran and Pontnewydd leaves the main line and as we pass over the junction there is a 5200 class tank waiting at the home signal with a loaded coal train waiting for us to clear. We're coming round on to a long straight stretch leading up to Pontypool and the Inspector tells me this is a fast stretch for down trains but that won't bother us as we are climbing up it. To the right is the rural peace of the Crown Estate at Llanfrechfa but to the left a whole new town is in the process of being built – Cwmbran – to rank with Harlow and Glenrothes as a new essay in model town planning. There's no doubt the area needs it, and from the amount of concrete and cranes involved its on a large scale – one wonders how it will turn out. There are factories to the left and the track stretches straight out before us. 4037 is steaming well and holding pressure steady at 215 with water at half a glass. Stan is lobbing choice lumps in to just the right spot in a deliberate fashion picking both his lump and where he wants to put it. Fred is puffing gently on his pipe, swaying with the motion of the engine with one hand resting on the brake handle and the other on the cabside. The Inspector and I are looking out at the countryside and for the moment all is as it should be. We're holding a steady 40 on the grade and there is no more anybody can do but let her 'make her way and take her time' as the Inspector says. The signals for Lower Pontnewydd are all off and we sail through and on the left we can now see Panteg Steelworks with our line rising up under an arched stone bridge, the final stretch into Pontypool Road. The gradient steepens slightly and as we pass up out of the cutting with our exhaust echoing across Griffithstown, we enter the busy world of Coedygric Junction with a large gasworks to the right and Pontypool Road depot and the junction for the Vale of Neath line to the left. Operations are in full swing here and there are engines everywhere, at the coal stage, in sidings and standing around the depot. The signals into Pontypool Road are clear and we now have to swing the train round a ninety-degree curve of the eastern leg of a triangular junction to get into the station. Fred gives her a little more on the screw having held her at 30% all the way from Llantarnam and as we pass the huge bay windowed Pontypool Road signal box under clear signals he eases her right back and lets her coast the rest of the way in. The platform at Pontypool Road will take a full fourteen coach train and as we are arriving slightly early Fred lets 4037 creep right to the end before bringing the whole lot to a stand with the tender within reach of the water column. It's a very neatly judged performance and the Inspector beams his approval.

Chapter 5
Scheme and Plot

PONTYPOOL ROAD is where passengers change for all South Wales destinations, and a whole phalanx leave the train with their luggage and depart for the connecting train, a Manchester-Swansea express behind 5008 'Raglan Castle' which is just running in on the other side of the island platform. A crush of passengers joins the train to replace those who left, and as Stan observes, he doesn't think we'll be any the lighter. Fred disappears with the oil feeder to check around and feel for heat. The Inspector is helping Stan fill the tender tank with water by operating the column valve and as I'm left standing there, I make myself useful by reaching over the tender coaming with the coal pick and pulling some coal forward. There's quite a precipice of it in front of me and with a few sharp tugs against the mass, about a quarter of a ton drops toward the shovel plate. It's mostly good stuff - big, close grained lumps, Markham and Bedwas mixed, the Inspector tells me - but we're starting to hit a lot of ovoids now and the quality of those is known to be patchy. Stan will have to avoid them if possible if we're not to have steaming trouble later. I pull with the pick at the large lumps of good coal I can see and quite a bit drops forward into the hole behind the shovel plate. Stan and the Inspector have finished taking water, and as Stan crosses the tender to return to the footplate he kicks a few choice lumps down into the hole. Getting me to pass the spare shovel up he quickly moves some of the larger lumps to where he can reach them and shifts some of the choicer stuff forward so that it will fall his way of its own accord later. Fred returns to the footplate, and says she's cool all round and beckons the Inspector and I to join him on the platform. He grabs the teacans and says he's off to the refreshment room for a refill as we've drunk the lot since Bristol, but Stan is going to give the fire a quick pull through with the fire irons, just to liven her up.

The fire irons are a good eight feet long and very heavy, and Stan has his work cut out to manhandle them up from the fireiron tunnel on his side of the cab and run them up and down the firebed to spread it around to his liking and break up any dead spots or clinker[11] he can see forming. I see the reason for caution when Stan pulls them out of the firebox and the end is almost white hot. You can't have several people and a man with a hot fire iron on the same footplate, which is why we are staying out of the way. Although we had a good fill on Undy troughs and we haven't come that far, the Inspector explains that with this train she's using about 50 gallons to the mile so even though there's plenty in the tank it seems you fill up wherever you can do so. Pontypool Road platform will take a full fourteen-coach train and allow us to have a fill. The platform at Hereford is shorter and will not take fourteen coaches all at once so we may have to pull up twice, hence we take water here, which should allow us to run all the way to Bromfield troughs at Ludlow where we should be able to fill the tank again. If they had been running a ten-coach train they may have gone through to Hereford and taken water there, but circumstances alter cases, and they're doing the prudent extra work now to save themselves trouble later on. It's not just the extra weight and length of a fourteen coach train he points out, but the fact that the journey must be planned and calculated in a different way. There's a great deal more to working steam trains than just a wide open regulator and hot fire, a lot of scheming and toil must go on to make it all happen in the right order at the right time, as I'm starting to find out.

Before we travel any further, lets look more closely at water. Common stuff, steam engines drink thousands of gallons of it and it is the bane of an engineman's life. They spend much of their time worrying about it, with the driver's eye watching the boiler water gauge and the fireman's watching the tender gauge at frequent intervals.

---

[11] Clinker was caused by slag like impurities in the coal which could fuse together and stop primary air coming through the firebars from the dampers down below. Depending on coal quality you either got a little or a lot and at the first opportunity you broke it up and got rid of it, or you may be short of steam later on. A curious blue-grey in colour when cool, Fred told me it was ideal for garden paths when broken down.

A dread is running short and having to make an out of course stop for more, or the cardinal sin of 'dropping a plug' if firebox water level becomes too low. So the rule is to take some at each and every reasonable opportunity. But there's more to it than that. Depending on the district you pass through, you may be consuming acid or alkali water governed by whether it is mountain or borehole water. Mountain water is generally purer and less likely to have suspended solids within it, especially if it has been softened. The best water is rainwater from upland catchments. Borehole or ground water usually has a lot of suspended solids, which have to be removed by treatment. This also breaks down into acid or alkali waters. Acid water wears out boilers and has to be treated to neutralise it and alkali water leaves a lot of sludge and scale, which has to be washed out at frequent intervals. Newly repaired locomotives were sometimes run-in in an alkali water district to put some sludge and scale on internal surfaces before transferring them back to their home depot which may be in an acid water district. The hope is that the one treatment will cancel out the effect of the other. Where the shopping and repair of locomotives is dictated by boiler condition then this becomes an important and expensive consideration. Locos in hard water districts with climbing curving lines suffer the worst wear and tear, while easily graded and relatively straight lines in soft water districts extend the life of a loco between shoppings. Locos are often reallocated from depots in hard water districts to soft water districts to try and avoid having a bulge in repairs at any one time. Water quality is carefully monitored and crews know of 'good' water columns and 'bad' ones where they will only stop to fill if the situation is desperate. A locomotive on heavy work like this one, will evaporate tons of water during a trip and the suspended solids precipitate out in the boiler as sludge and have to be washed out at frequent intervals. If the boiler is not washed out to schedule then steaming capacity suffers as the solids build up. The best case is a locomotive having ample supplies of unpolluted rainwater for its boiler feed. There will be no scale, less suspended solids so extending the time between washouts and less need for re-tubes as a result of scaled up boiler tubes.

4037 has tablets of a water treatment chemical called 'Alfloc' added to the tender water and some were thrown in to the tank at Pontypool. This dissolves in the feed water and prevents foaming in the boiler and helps to keep heating surfaces clear of sludge. Foaming can cause that other engineman's dread of water being carried over, past the regulator valve, through the superheater and into the cylinders where damage could ensue. Impure water can also cause steaming problems which can miraculously disappear once a few tenderfuls of good clean stuff are taken on. Water is great deal more subtle in these circumstances than its appearance may suggest.

Fred returns with teacans filled as Stan is restowing the fireirons in their tunnel on the running board. I commented that he hadn't been long, but he said the crowd in the refreshment room parts like the Red Sea when enginemen carrying teacans turn up and the ladies behind the counter always put their cans straight under the urn. Enginemen never use boiler water for making tea, but en-route they know all the points where tea cans can be refilled, and if stopped in the country they always pull up at a signal box. A few hundredweight of coal for full teacans is the going rate, and the signalmen never go cold and they never go thirsty. It's called the balance of trade he said and helps oil the wheels of commerce.

It's been non-stop action during this station stop until now, as far as we are concerned, although we have only been here seven minutes. A man in overalls carrying a long handled hammer and what appears to be a watering can except that it has an oil spout appears at track level. The Pontypool Road wheel tapper has been down the offside of the train testing tyres and feeling bearings for heat. He gives us the nod so all must be well with no obvious defects in carriage underframes or running gear. Long distance trains get examined at a number of places as a matter of course, and this man, as well as tapping tyres and feeling bearings is looking for anything loose or dragging in our train. If a defect had been found, then the offending carriage would have been shunted out of the train there and then, and sent for repair. Its another facet of safe working of trains that would pass unnoticed to all but the knowledgeable observer. Across in the adjoining bay platform are two locomotives, an LM Region 'Patriot' 45524 'Blackpool' and standing behind it a Western Region Hall class 5948 'Siddington Hall'. Both engines are reasonably clean in lined green livery, and appear to have had the steam pipe run over their wheels and running gear to remove the worst of the dust and dirt. The 'Patriot' is co-incidentally waiting to take over an excursion from Swansea to Blackpool, which is currently travelling over the Vale of Neath line and the Hall, is waiting for a troop special from Okehampton to Oswestry. Both will depart within twenty minutes of us, so we will have to run hard to stay out of their way. Both engines have Pontypool crews who will work them through to Shrewsbury. The 'Patriot' will be handed over to a LM crew at Shrewsbury while the Hall will be handed over to a set of Shrewsbury men to be worked on to Gobowen on the Chester line. That's what they told us, and they were highly amused to see Stan 'slaving for this Salop feller' as one put it. He was given much advice, from a distance, while cleaning the fire and both firemen said they were better off keeping out of his way while all the white hot stuff was going on, but they were happy to lend moral support from their respective cabs. The presence of ex-LMS locomotives explains the attraction of Pontypool Road to the crowd of engine spotters who are on the platform and also observing operations from the approach road embankment near the station, which provides a fine grandstand. The LMR engines travelling south, are often changed at Pontypool Road for ex-GW ones and a variety of 'foreign' types find their way here, including some of Crewe's freshly overhauled ones from time to time. The mix of motive power makes for great enthusiast interest, but as a result Pontypool's crews have had to become adept at working ex-LMS locomotives in addition to the native ones, even though the Midland engines are driven and fired from the opposite side. This must make life interesting as the sighting of signals and landmarks is totally different when driving say a Midland 'Royal Scot' compared to a 'Castle', and a Pontypool engineman could end up handling both types within the same shift.

One advantage of Pontypool's huge platform is that it is long and straight and you can see what's going on. The Swansea train on the other side, whistles and stamps away under the bridge with

'Raglan Castle' getting it's ten coaches away in sharp,classic style. The open doors of our train are starting to shut and it looks like all are aboard who want to be aboard. A wedding party appears about five coaches back and a knot of people are at the doors talking and hugging. There's a wave from the signal box near us and the clang of the starter dropping to clear means its almost time to be off. The water level is near the top of the glass and pressure has climbed to 220, and 4037 is starting to hum to herself again. Stan pulls the firehole flap up to protect his trousers and boots, and Fred leans out and looks back along the platform waiting for the off. The wedding party is thinning out and making final farewells, porters are checking doors and far down the train we see a glint of sunshine on chrome plate as our guard brings his whistle up and blows a long shrill blast followed by a flash of green. We've seen it, but Fred waits momentarily to see it repeated by the platform inspector half way down before letting out a long shriek on the whistle.

The rest happens quickly. Ejector open to evacuate the brakes, four twists on the screw to put her in forward gear, and a heave of the regulator upwards, and 4037 eases ahead and starts to speak. Deep slow, heavy blasts from the stack, rattling the windows in Pontypool North Box as we heave our train away and onto the downgrade that takes us eventually to the bridge over the River Usk at The Bryn where the hard work will really begin.

Chapter 6
The Drover's Town

AS WE curve away on the downgrade, the signals ahead are clear and speed is starting to rise. Fred notches her up as the train is running well behind and there no point in tearing up the fire yet. Stan looks back down the train for the guard's wave that all is well, and then quickly puts eight shovelfuls into her while she's chattering contentedly along, and straightening up catches the wave of the signalman at Little Mill Junction. Incidentally, this is not just people being friendly, even though railway people get to know each other by sight, a wave from the box means 'As far as I can see, you are in good order, with no open doors and nothing dragging'. Any frantic hand movement, other than a wave is interpreted as 'Stop'. The Rule Book also says something about firemen being disengaged when passing signal boxes, and Stan has observed this to the letter as part of his pattern of work.

Little Mill used to be the junction for the branch to Monmouth and Usk, closed since 1955 except for a section to Glascoed, and this beautiful line veers off through the trees to the right. Stan starts playing a tune on the whistle and crossing to Fred's side as we pass the British Nylon Spinners factory at Mamhilad they are both looking intently ahead. The reason becomes clear. Two small children and a young woman standing by the fence near a row of houses waving madly. Stan's wife and children come to see him at work. We all start waving and theres 'Half a pound of tuppeny rice' played on the whistle as we roar by, whistling and waving until they are out of sight. Fred is chuckling to himself, saying that his used to do that when they were young. It takes him back he says. We've come to the bottom of the grade from Pontypool Road and there's a short stiff climb up at 1 in 141 to a crest just before Nantyderry. With the momentum gathered on the descent from Pontypool and the fast moving weight of fourteen coaches behind us, Fred need only give 4037 a breath more of steam to take us sailing over it at near 70. Stan crosses to his side as we pass under the aqueduct in Nantyderry cutting and continues building up the fire. She's showing a full glass at just under blowing off point and we're running steadily downgrade at 65. Fred's got her on an easy rein and letting her run just in front of the train heeling easily to the curves. Nantyderry distant is off and the old stone station with the signalbox on the platform comes in sight. The platforms here are staggered under an overbridge and as we speed through with a warning shriek on the whistle, the signalman waves from the platform where he is talking with a farmer who is unloading bagged fertiliser from a wagon in the goods yard. It's a peaceful sunny Saturday at Nantyderry and a passing express is a momentary distraction.

To the left is the huge mass of the Blorenge mountain that continues the rampart of hills that form the Welsh Valleys and to the east the lush farmland of the Vale of Usk, with its well appointed white washed farms and cottages and beautifully kept fields. The Blorenge down as far as Pontypool has now been incorporated into the Brecon Beacons National Park, which takes in nearly all of southern Breconshire and part of north Monmouthshire and seeks to preserve the stunning landscapes from unsightly development and for future generations. All of this was announced in 1955, and Stan tells me that it has led to an increase in wealthy people 'from away' buying homes in the area, and that Abergavenny has become the destination of many walkers and ramblers that we see on the summer trains in this area and on hills and lanes as we pass.

It's 1 in 80 down to the crossing of the Usk at the Bryn, which is the lowest point of this part of the line. Unfortunately there is a 50 restriction over the river bridge here which means that the climb from there to Llanvihangel starts with a handicap which is compounded by the stop at Abergavenny and the need for a banker on restarting. Any hope of using the momentum of the train for a flying start up the grade is nullified and from the Bryn onwards to Llanvihangel its all 'against the collar' as Fred puts it. Stan is still steadily putting good lump coal just where he wants it, and with her white hot fire and showing a half a glass of water, a steady rubbing of the brakes brings us down to the specified 50 as we cross the river.

There are some boys paddling in the shallows here, and from the fish we can see twitching on the grass, they are engaged in 'tickling' trout, from the voids just below the river's bank. The Usk is renowned in angling circles for the quality of its fish and the Inspector tells me that during rationing, the 'tickling' of trout, an old poachers art, was a highly prized skill, and commanded a premium on the black market. Fred shoots him a quizzical sideways glance and removing his pipe for a moment says 'Not that you would know anything about that, Boss?' and raises a theatrical eyebrow,' When was the last time you ate trout you actually paid for?' he says with a grin. Stan starts to laugh, and as we whistle and give the lads a wave, they are just sending another occupant of the Usk flying through the air to flounder on the bank. 'Used to do it myself', says Stan, 'but there's a better spot just up there below Llanellen', pointing upriver in the direction of Abergavenny.

Coming off the river bridge past the old church and its graveyard, theres the small village of Penpergwm basking in the sunshine, and passing the box and the closed station we are now on the lower reaches of the climb up the sides of the Usk valley that will take us to Llanvihangel, or 'Laughing Angel' as our crew have it. Fred gives a code on the whistle, known as a 'crow' to let the Abergavenny signalman know he will need the banker and as he opens the regulator right up and gives 4037 40% on the screw we hit the climb with a vengeance and she settles down to a full throated steady four cylinder roar that must echo right across to Llanover and Llanellen on the opposite bank.

The view ahead from the footplate is beautiful. The blue-green summer colour of the Blorenge is on the left with the farms and villages of Llanover, Llanfoist and Llanellen crouched at its base. There are coppices and farmland stretched out around us looking like a manicured model landscape and in front is the bulk of the Sugar Loaf mountain, 1,955 ft, towering over the old drovers town of Abergavenny, which is now the gateway to the Brecon Beacons National Park. From here to Pontrilas we will skirt the National Park and it's one of the most scenic stretches of main line in Britain. The whole train is on the grade now and speed is being held to a steady 50 and with the roar from the chimney, she's holding two thirds of a glass of water against the injector at a steady 220 on the clock Stan has got things more or less as he wants them and there's no more he can do for now, as we're shortly to stop at Abergavenny anyway.

Roaring towards Abergavenny, passing the very tall distant signals we pass the box and dozing by the goods shed is our banker, a '7200' class 2-8-2 tank, 7225, and not very long out of the shops judging by her glossy black condition. Two Ponty men are gazing from the footplate back down our train, and seeing Stan comments are made,as we sweep by to coast gently into Abergavenny (Monmouth Road). Until a few years ago Abergavenny had three stations, Monmouth Road, Abergavenny Junction and Brecon Road, but the closure of the old Merthyr, Tredegar and Abergavenny line with it's spectacular gradients in 1958 led to Brecon Road and the Junction closing and all traffic is now handled at Monmouth Road which is the old Great Western station, since Abergavenny Junction used to be the LMS one. Running in past the station building there's quite a crowd waiting for this train and we will have to draw on well up the platform so that the '72' can get out of the goods loop and buffer up behind. To do this we have to draw right up to the starter signal to get as much of the train alongside the platform as we can. As we come to a stand, we are on the lower reaches of a curving 1 in 85 grade with the train stretched out along the curved platform behind. Getting away cleanly from here will be both noisy and difficult, even with the '72' pushing most of the weight behind.

Chapter 7
The Abergavenny Banker

WAITING in the sunshine at Abergavenny, standing well past the platform end, Fred reaches up above his head and takes down the two large pasties he put up there at Temple Meads. He had wrapped them in newspaper as well as the greaseproof, and in the shareout both he and Stan break off large chunks and hand them to us. Tea is poured and ease is taken for a moment. 4037 is hot and ready to go, the sun is shining on our backs, and the homemade Devon pastie and tea taste wonderful. 'Take your time', says Fred, 'we let him do most of the work to Llanvihangel, so this is where we eat - we'll have no time later.'

Stan climbs up on the tender end using a convenient footstep and holding on to the cab roof and tender coaming is able to see back down the platform over the roofs of the carriages. At the end of the train, by the footbridge he can see 7225 starting to blow off ready for the coming fray. We are standing near to the buildings of Pen-y-fal Hospital and the Inspector points out the rooms that Rudolf Hess was kept in during the War. Apparently he used to see him walking in the lanes around Abergavenny and Llanvihangel with his Military Police escort while he was working trains through the area. A very friendly man he said, he always waved at engine crews and they used to keep an eye out for him. It wasn't every day you got to see Hitler's deputy in the flesh especially during those years.

The '72' gives a 'crow' on the whistle, which Fred answers, Stan looks back along the train and then swings down under the cab roof. 'Right Away' he says nodding across to Fred. During the stop they had decided that my footplate education must be extended by a spell of firing, just to tell my grandchildren (when I have some to tell) that I had done it. The flap is dropped and the firedoors closed for now and as we feel 7225 compressing the train behind us Fred evacuates the brake and heaves open the regulator. With cutoff already set to 60% 4037 gives a sneeze from the

snifting valves and moves forward, with very little fuss. After
several revolutions Fred gives her some more steam and she
really starts to speak. He is only interested in the first seven
coaches he says, let the banker push the rest. He's not coupled to
the train, as per the Appendix instructions, so he'll drop back as
our last coach passes Llanvihangel box, get crossed to the down
line and run back down to bank another train up the hill.

Stan shows me how and where to stand, and on his instruction I
begin. Slide shovel under coal, loading tip of same, keeping hold of
handle reach across with other hand and open firehole doors, pull
loaded shovel out from under coal and bringing other hand to its
handle swing round bent half low, and pitch the shovelful into the
fire in just the right place. Don't let go of shovel handle whatever
you do, as you'll be neither the first nor last to have thrown a
shovel in the fire. Steam trains can't go anywhere without a
shovel, which is why there is always a spare (or two) carried on
jobs like this. A loose shovel handle is dangerous so if that
develops its always best to have another one handy. Swinging
from the fire in one movement slide the shovel back under the coal
ready to repeat the minuet, and remember, your stance does not
change during the whole process. The moment you start shifting
feet doing this you can be pitched across the footplate by a sudden
lurch, so you pick your spot and swing from the waist like a PT
instructor. Its easier when she's pulling on the grade as
everything is stretched out taut and she's not pitching and
banging, it's a lot harder on the downhill stretches where she's
pitching, rolling and banging unpredictably with the surging
forces of the following train acting on the tender.

I have to keep on firing her to Stan's liking to the top of
Llanvihangel Bank, so he starts to give me a running commentary
telling me exactly where to put each shovelful. 'Under the door',
'two in the left middle', 'four in each back corner'. I've got my head
down, and turning, lifting, swinging and pitching, I am starting to
work to a rhythm. My shoulders and the small of my back are
starting to ache and I've only been at it for a few minutes. We've
passed Abergavenny Junction and looking across I can see the old

church at Llantilio Pertholey slumbering in the sunshine. The Inspector is watching me and giving advice on technique and Stan is maintaining his trainer's patter. Fred is highly amused, pipe between his teeth, looking ahead with the odd glance back on the curves to see how the banker is doing. 4037 is holding up well with pressure at 215 and the water level steady at just over half a glass. Fred has wound her back to 30% to lessen the pull on the fire and keep boiler demand steady. Stan quickly sets the exhaust injector and the water level is starting to climb back up as I continue swinging and shovelling to the exhausts beat as she battles the heavy grade up the slopes of Skirrid Fawr. Back in the train, people are probably looking out, talking, dozing or eating in the restaurant car, only barely aware of all the noise and din involved in getting up the hill in time. Straightening my back and leaning on the shovel for a moment, I looked across to see a large house in immaculately tended grounds, and there is a charming little vignette. A family group of six are reclining in deck chairs on the lawn and looking across at us. One lifts a glass filled with amber liquid, and Fred gives him a few short blasts on the whistle in acknowledgement and a wave back. They must have heard us coming from Abergavenny, with the noise we are making and the two children in the group are counting the following coaches and waving at the people in the train. Stan says he sees them there quite often in the summer and has seen the children grow from afar over the years. I said it was nice to sit on your front lawn with live theatre laid on every so often. He says that they must be shrewd observers of form and from our sound and progress up the hill would have known exactly how we were doing long before we came in sight.

(Many years later, at a dinner in another European country I met a lady who had lived in a house overlooking the line at Abergavenny as a child in the 1950's. She confirmed the truth of Stan's comment and said that she used to watch the train engines and bankers tackling the hill at night, fascinated by the flashing firelights, and the noise and drama of steam trains going about their business in the small hours. Many times she would see the crews silhouetted in the cabs by the light of the fire, or the fireman in mid swing with a shovel full of coal. She said you could track events from the whistling of the bank engine and train engine at Abergavenny, its progress, strident or otherwise up the hill, the banker dropping away at the summit and then finally the sound of the banker clanking light-heartedly back down the hill for another pushing session. She was often lulled to sleep by the sounds of steam engines climbing to Llanvihangel and to this day retains a fondness for steam trains even though she would never call herself an enthusiast. To her, the sound of steam engines working at night, carried on the clear, still air signified a safe, secure world of order and purpose, quite unlike the frenetic chaos we seem to be surrounded by today - her words not mine.)

Back to work as we swing through mountain pasture onto a series of curves below Llanvihangel, and each shovelful onto the now white fire is answered by a grey discolouration at the stack of a clear exhaust. She's climbing hard and steadily and feels if she's slightly accelerating, so the banker must be doing a good job.

Matters are looking healthy and we appear to be gaining on the booked timing according to Fred who is doing rapid mental calculation with his watch. She's rasping away at the chimney top and pressure and water level are holding steady at 215 and two thirds of a glass with an incandescent white fire and doing about 20. I'm feeling rather pleased with myself and Stan maintains his running commentary while I fire steadily to his instruction. He tells me to watch the water disappear down the glass as we go over the top at Llanvihangel, which is why we are carrying two thirds of a glass now with the injector singing away. Steam crews were always wary of any possibility of the boiler water level getting dangerously low and dropping a fusible plug. Fusible plugs were lead-filled safety devices in the top of the firebox which would blow through in the event of a low water level and at least give some warning of a danger, no matter what the water gauge was actually showing. It has been known for gauges to get partially blocked with scale, even though they are thoroughly cleaned out at boiler washouts, so the fusible plugs were there as a final warning. Enginemen always inspected them on taking over a locomotive at a changeover point, and always checked water gauges as a matter of course. At no time on the journey was water level allowed to fall to the bottom third of the glass, it was expertly kept within the upper two thirds, no matter what the changes of grade, and at no time was the glass absolutely full of water, so avoiding the other enginemen's bete noir of water carried over into the cylinders, also known as 'priming' which could wash away lubrication and in extreme cases lead to cylinder damage as water is incompressible. This demanded great skill and an intimate knowledge of the route and gradients and unless the observer's attention had been drawn to it could have passed unnoticed. It was and is part of the fine art of working steam traction that has almost been lost down the years.

On the curve below Llanvihangel, Stan looks in the box and says 'That's enough' so I slide the shovel under the coal and straighten up, sweaty and aching. 'Nice swing' says Fred, removing his pipe,'you could have done it for a living.' My palms are sore and my back is aching. My knee joints feel like jelly and I've only been doing this for a few minutes. Stan tells me I'm too tense and to relax my knees slightly like a small boat sailor. 'You have to get into the rhythm of the machine', he says 'or she'll jar you to death. The important thing with a steam loco is to stay on top of it, and fire little and often, and to a set pattern. The minute you get lazy, lose concentration and start putting it in any old how things will go wrong, especially with this sort of load, so you watch the fire, steam, water and road like a hawk' and 'anticipatory action is the name of the game', a phrase which has been a sound doctrine in many situations since.

We're passing the end of the Llanvihangel siding and up above us is the brake van of a long freight behind Pontypool's 2807 which has been backed into the refuge and awaits our passing. Stan greets colleagues as we jog past them and through Llanvihangel. This summit station has a small box in the cutting and staggered platforms with a private waiting room up on the left hand side which is now a cottage, but the station is shut so no walkers or shoppers are awaiting the local train. Over the top, with a wave from the solitary figure in the box, and as the banker drops away speed starts to rise rapidly on the 1in 100 downgrade beyond the cutting. The water level in our boiler changes markedly on the down slope and we begin to rapidly accelerate as the weight of the train falls in behind. The regulator is left where it is and Fred winds the reverser back to 20% and lets her make her way. From barely 20 a few minutes ago we are now up to 70 and rising, with 14 packed coaches leaning on the tender. She's flying over the ground on the first bit of good downhill running since Nantyderry. Pandy distant signal is off, and the ATC bell is ringing happily so we're for a clear run through this section at least. On the long curves down the valley Fred leaves her where she is and is standing braced against the roll of the cab like a sailing ship skipper with smoking pipe in one hand and the other resting on the brake handle. His eyes never leave the road ahead. Stan drops the flap and puts four good shovel full's into the box in the right places and waits for the grey smoke to clear over the tender, then adds another four. This keeps her happy and hot and speed rises to 85. The Black Mountains stand, full of foreboding, on the left – no wonder the Romans and everyone since left the Welsh tribes alone - and to the right are the cleft bulk of Skirrid Fawr and the hills of south Herefordshire. All signals are off and Pandy comes into view, a small attractive station, but closed now for over two years. Fred gives a long warning blast on the whistle as we are now travelling at over 90 and the signalman in Pandy box raises a hand in acknowledgement as we tear through, a blizzard of straw, sweet papers and ballast dust rising in our wake. We must make an impressive sight bearing down on him with the train stretched out around the curve, a clean engine with a smokeless stack and a blossom showing at the safety valves, being hard worked under a summer sky. How many times has he seen this I wonder? I catch a glimpse of two children – a boy and a girl – open mouthed, standing at the window in the outside corner of the box, looking on in avid fascination and behind them, the signalman reaching up to his block instruments to pass us on to his colleague at Pontrilas – and then the cameo is gone, our huge noisy train rushing through and on into the countryside to leave them with the crake of the pheasant and the bleating of the sheep in their beautiful setting.

Pandy station was the home at one time of the author Raymond Williams who wrote of people of the Black Mountains and was a

Professor of English at Cambridge University. His father was one of Pandy's signalmen, and young Raymond Williams must have seen expresses like this rush through Pandy many times in his youth, and possibly from the same signal box window.

Chapter 8
Trouble at Tram Inn

A FARMER and his sheepdog both stop and look as they cross a field in the sunshine, to take in the sight of a very long, fast moving express train and it's well kept 'Castle'. The farmer almost instinctively raises a hand and we answer with the whistle, - the dog just looks dumbstruck. The Inspector points out a small church near the river with a very old half-timbered tower, which he tells me, are a feature of the area. 4037 is starting a gentle nosing motion now on the reverse curves below Llangua , and as Inspector Lewis looks across Fred has already sensed it and his hand on the brake takes a few inches of vacuum out of the trainpipe. This is enough to tighten the train against the lunging of 4037, and with fourteen coaches acting as a damper and a leash, she settles down to steady fast running as we pass the Pontrilas distant signal at clear. Careering on, round the reverse curves and crossing the Monnow at Monmouth Cap two fishermen look up and raise a hand in greeting. The fire is white hot and hurtful and Stan puts a few shovelfuls over the flap to keep her sweet , turns the blower on half a turn and shuts the firedoors for Pontrilas tunnel to keep the flames in the box. 4037 heels to the curve with the train roaring behind and we give a long shrill whistle and dive into the short bore.

Pontrilas station is on the other side drenched in sunshine, and whistling to warn two trainspotters on the platform,we rocket through. A light engine is standing in the loop outside the signal box – 3862, a Collett 2-8-0 , pointing north - and the crew on the footplate together with the signalman standing on the box steps, look on in awe as we flash through, raising a storm of dust, old straw and chicken feathers on the unswept platform of this now closed station. The tall, ancient wooden signal box (still in use in 2006!) has all windows open on this very hot day, and from a glance at the frame all signals are off as we run through, past the junction for the Golden Valley line to Hay, and into the short climb up towards St.Devereaux.   We're running well on the slightly rising grade and we're doing 60 on the short level stretch through the hop fields south of Kilpeck, when we see St. Devereaux distant on with the home signal off. In the distance a man with an orange flag is walking towards us in the cess at the side of the line. Something is amiss. Fred opens the blower and shuts off, braking steadily and gradually using the vacuum ejector against the brake, watching the trainpipe gauge, and creating and destroying vacuum to bring us smoothly down to a fast walking pace. The Inspector crosses to Stan's side and leans out as we approach the walking figure, who appears to be a signal lineman. As we approach he very deftly moves closer, towards the sleeper ends, and as we pass him and the cab comes level he scrambles up onto our lower footsteps on the cess side and comes up to stand in the cab entrance. ' Cows on the line at Tram Inn - go careful'. The Inspector acknowledges this and passes the news on to Fred, who gives 4037 some full regulator to take us up towards St.Devereaux box at the top of a short rise. As we start to bark up the hill a detonator goes off under our wheels making me jump in fright. Everybody, including our visitor, has a good laugh at this. 'I thought I would shoot you as well in case you didn't see me in the cess'. It would have been difficult to miss him with the flag he was carrying and the number of eyes aboard, but he didn't know that and had acted as per the regulations and placed one a quarter mile from the box and was hurrying to place one half a mile away when we picked him up. Fred shuts off again a few hundred yards short of the box and lets the speed run out so that we are barely crawling along. The signalman leans well out of the box window and shouts across 'Cows at Tram Inn ' and shows us an orange flag. Our lineman drops neatly off onto the platform and Stan gives him a wave of acknowledgement as Fred opens up to accelerate us steadily up the rest of the grade. Not once did we stop, and the rolling momentum of fourteen coaches was not broken. Still rasping along over the top we are into a dip where we pick up speed and then out of that on to the level where we've got back up to about 40. We're tramping along trying to regain momentum and as we approach Tram Inn a platelayer with a large orange flag is standing on the trackside verge waving steadily. We whistle in acknowledgement and Fred eases her down to coast along. As we pass the platelayer another detonator goes off under our wheels. A few hundred yards away we can see a boy and two platelayers herding cows to an accommodation crossing and back into a lineside field. They're safely out of the way now, but the caution was justified, and as we pass, the platelayers, boy and the conscripted crew of a looped freight are busy coaxing them further up the field away from the gateway.A train hitting a herd of cows makes an astounding mess according to the Inspector and has been known to cause derailments. 'It'd be vets, police and buckets of blood if we'd hit that lot' he said - nodding in their direction.

The Tram Inn signalman is showing a green flag and all signals are off so we will attempt to recover some running time in the six miles to Hereford. Fred opens her up wide and gives her 55% on the screw and we start to stamp angrily away along the level to get up to a respectable 55 as we hit the 1 in 300 rise up to Haywood Lodge. Fred keeps her hard at it up the hill, and Stan has stopped firing for now and pulled up the flap. We'll coast downhill into Hereford from Haywood Tunnel and shutting the injector off he wants to run down the water level so that she will stand quiet at Hereford, our next booked stop, as he refills the boiler. We're running past orchards and hop fields now, both heavy with fruit and the large brick and half-timbered farmhouses are starting to get more numerous. We've entered the prosperous farming country of South Herefordshire and ahead is the short tunnel at Haywood Lodge, beyond which is Red Hill Junction. We've now hit the downgrade into Hereford and Fred lets speed rise to a steady 60 at which he eases her and lets her coast. Whistling through the short tunnel, which is more like a long overbridge we veer right at Red Hill Junction and onto the downhill stretch of 1 in 92 that takes us around the south side of Hereford down to the Wye River Bridge. Standing on the relief lines leading into Hereford at Red Hill are several freight trains nose to tail, waiting for their paths to the south. This has been common for years the Inspector tells me, and they are allowed to do it due to a permissive block system on the Hereford avoiding line. They will be released one after the other, once southbound paths become available between the procession of expresses and long distance relief trains that pass this way on a summer Saturday. I'm told that during the last War it was not unusual to be waiting here for up to eight hours if you were the last freight in a queue on this line, and it was quite possible for a driver and firemen to relieve a crew at Hereford shed, move the train two miles and then get relieved after eight hours without the train having moved beyond Red Hill Junction. It only gets remotely like that now on summer Saturdays, like today. The wartime period was very trying for engine crews with rationing, long hours, the blackout and air raids to contend with as well as over utilised locomotives and it was several years after the War before arrears of maintenance in track ,locos and stock were recovered. All agree that the last ten years have been the best they can remember but they say that maintenance of steam locomotives is starting to suffer due to staff shortages and the coming of the diesels, which are absorbing a lot of the railway's technical manpower due to their reliability problems.

The strange thing is that the steam locomotive will keep going stubbornly on even though diesels seem to suffer strange minor faults that turn them into a non-runner perhaps blocking a route until they can be removed. This is why we are seeing so many steam pilot engines at major traffic centres apparently; to substitute for failed diesels after dragging them out of the way.

Running easily downhill towards Rotherwas Junction at the foot of the grade the train is strung out around the long curve and looking back droplights and compartment windows are open with faces at many of them. It's a beautiful day and running on through the warm air many are enjoying the weather. There's a large army base on the left hand side which they tell me is the headquarters of the Special Air Service, and clattering over Rotherwas Junction and past the box we run over the Wye river bridge and past the back gardens of the outer suburbs of Hereford. The signals are all clear and as we approach Ayleston Hill distant signal it drops to clear and we give an answering whistle in acknowledgement. There are some sidings to the left that are being used to hold carriages and a diesel multiple unit which is ticking over quietly in the sunshine.

A short train of four coaches headed up by a beautifully clean Churchward 2-6-0 no. 7312 is standing in the sidings beyond. The Mogul is lined out in passenger lining as well and in its immaculate condition looks a sight for sore eyes. The Inspector tells me those engines were plain green or black for years and it was only in 1956/57 that they started to be painted green and lined out in passenger livery, and how well it suits them. The crew are taking their ease in the cutaway cab, the driver standing, drinking a cup of tea raises a hand as he sees us but the fireman has his head in what appears to be the Daily Mirror. They are running behind us as the connection from this train to Leominster, Woofferton, Ludlow, Craven Arms and Church Stretton, to save us stopping at these places. They will move into the Hereford platform as we leave and will run about five minutes behind. Fred says he intends to show them a clean pair of heels as far as Leominster, and after that it won't matter as the margin will get greater. Speed has run out to just over 30, and we pass under a road bridge and curve sharply to the left into Hereford Barrs Court station, past Ayleston Hill box. and running along a crowded platform, Fred lets the momentum run out as the train follows us through the pointwork and with a virtuoso application of the brake brings speed down to gently halt next to Hereford Station signal box.

Chapter 9
The Fire Bucket and its uses...

HEREFORD has a handsome red brick station in the local vernacular, which is a sort of Tudor style with many chimneys. There's quite a lot going on here, 4136 with Gloucester train at the opposite platform is just leaving and in the bay is 46512 waiting with a train for Hay-on-Wye, Three Cocks, Talgarth and Brecon. Another 'Castle' number 5018 'St.Mawes Castle' stands at the far platform with a chocolate and cream liveried train for the Malvern's, Worcester and eventually London. This is the 'Cathedrals Express'. Cardiff's 70029 'Shooting Star' creeps past us as we run in just arriving with a 12-coach southbound Manchester – Paignton train. Hereford's up platform will not take a full fourteen coach train, which means the rear van is standing back out under the road overbridge at the station throat. Once the initial rush of passengers is over we will have to pull up to get the rear van alongside the platform for luggage to be unloaded. This can be a fraught operation on a crowded platform, so the platform inspector and the train guard are closely supervising the whole thing. Since the water level had been run down on the descent from Haywood Lodge, Stan is quietly refilling the boiler to the three-quarter level by using the live steam injector rather than the exhaust steam version. The live steam injector takes cold water from the tender and uses direct live steam from the boiler to both warm and inject the water into the boiler. It cools things more than the exhaust steam injector and since the blower is on and the fire still packing a sting it will help keep her quiet without wasteful blowing off while we shunt the train. Taking the opportunity, Stan hoses down the footplate and tender front to clean everything up and lay some dust, as the pep pipe only works when the injectors are running. Shutting this and the injector off as water level is regained Stan takes a quick look round to see that all is clean and tidy and disappears with the teacan.

Porters are shutting doors and blowing whistles, and on a hand signal from the platform inspector we draw slowly forward about three coach lengths, taking the engine past the signal box to stand beyond, but with the rear of the train now spotted for loading, but it means we are past the starter signal so the start will be made on a flag signal from the adjacent box.   Stan reappears with the refilled teacan from the refreshment room and an 'acquired' Hereford station fire bucket full of sand. This is put to stand in the front corner of the cab on the fireman's side. Stan notices my quizzical look, and putting an index finger up and tapping the side of his nose says 'Watch', and nothing else.

While waiting for the off Fred proceeded to shut down and drain the sight feed lubricator on the back of the boiler. First he took a steel bottle of oil which had been standing in his corner of the cab and put it on the shelf over the firehole door, where it would warm nicely. Then, explaining to me what he was doing, he shut off the steam supply to the lubricator, and then opened the drain from the lubricator into a waste pipe. By watching this he could see when the steam and water began to be replaced by oil. A fair amount of water was forced out, as it was still under pressure and as soon as oil started to spit through he shut the drain. Taking a large spanner which he had got from the tender toolbox, he slackened the brass filling plug in the top of the lubricator and this allowed the remainder of the pressure within it to escape with a gentle 'Pfrrrrtttt!!'

With the plug out, there's a gauze filter that he removes to check for dirt and then replaces. Taking the warmed oil bottle from the firehole tray he shows me some of the oil he's about to add. Its known as 'Black Jack' but its official name is 'Superheater Oil' and is made for use at high temperatures. It's very thick and is like pouring treacle, even though its been warmed. He slowly pours the oil into the lubricator, leaving about a three-quarter of an inch space at the top. Then he refits and tightens the filling plug and reopens the steam supply. She's now got enough oil to take her through to Shrewsbury.

There are four feeds on the lubricator, and the ones for the cylinders have been set to supply a droplet of oil through the sight glass about three times a minute. This is usually enough for most classes of work he tells me, but since its only about 50 miles to Shrewsbury and he's just filled the lubricator he reckons to increase the feed a little more as the hardest work of the trip is about to begin. I said I thought the climb to Llanvihangel was onerous enough but he says the climb to Church Stretton proceeds in a number of steps and begins in earnest up at Dinmore Tunnel, and for the next thirty miles to Little Stretton Halt there will be very little respite apart from some short downhill stretches on the way up, as the line follows the prevailing contours. She'll have to be hit hard to keep the running times and get to the top without trouble as with this weight and length of train there is little or no margin for error.

Standing over in the yard, two tracks away is a '2251' class small 0-6-0 tender engine No. 2241 of a type used on secondary and branch lines. This too, is in lined out green livery and looks very spick and span. This one has a small tender attached allowing me to see into the cab, and looking across, the fireman appears to be cracking eggs into the shovel. Fred tells me there's nothing wrong with my eyes, they're just having a grand fry up during a break in shunting. They can't do it on fast passenger work, but on freight and shunting work where they may be standing in refuges and other sidings for a while, it is the practice to fry food on the shovel. Its not as unhygienic as you might think. The hot water hose ('pep pipe') on the footplate is first used to scald the shovel blade, and the bacon is put on. The shovel with the bacon is then held inside the firehole doors, over the mound of coal usually built up there. As this fries in its own fat and greases the shovel, the shovel is then withdrawn and the other ingredients of the full English breakfast are arranged. You can add to taste, eggs, mushrooms, tomatoes, sausages and bread for fried bread. All can be put on the shovel blade which is like a large skillet, easily taking enough to feed two hungry men, and in holding it just inside the firedoor the intense heat fries the food in its own juices very quickly. Fred tells me you will taste no finer breakfast anywhere, especially if you are held in some wayside loop line at 5 a.m. on a dark, cold winter's morning waiting for expresses to pass you by. He and Stan bought pasties for today because there would be no opportunity for a fry, but when they are on work that calls for a lot of standing in sidings, a supply of food is taken along and at the right time they cook it fresh. He tells me he has cooked braised steak and onions on top of the condenser coil before now. The trick is to wrap the steak and chopped onion in greaseproof paper followed by newspaper, just like fish and chips and then put it on top of the coil. About half way through the shift, you and it will be ready for each other he says, and it will be cooked to perfection. Baked potatoes can also be done by putting potatoes behind the steam valves on the manifold that is fixed to the top of the boiler in the cab roof. After a few hours all you need is a knife, fork and some butter and away you go. As he says, there's no need to go hungry or thirsty on this job if you know what you are doing. The fireman on the '22' takes the shovel out of the firebox and his driver is there in a flash waving two mess tins. The bacon, egg, fried bread and tomatoes are put into the mess tins very quickly and the two chefs disappear down the offside of the engine to find somewhere quiet and less public to eat. Fred says that people generally don't believe them when they say they cook food on the shovel, but at the smell of a thick toasted bacon sandwich wafting from the cab on a cold morning all cynicism usually disappears.

The blower is 'cracked' on to keep a steady haze at the chimney top and Stan is flicking the odd small shovelful into just the right places while she's standing. A platform inspector appears beside the cab at floor level 'We'll get you away shortly driver, you'll be non-stop to Salop. We're just clearing the last van. You'll get the tip from the box', meaning we'll get the right away passed by a handsignal or flag from the signalman in Hereford station box, which we are well beyond. The rear two thirds of the train is now standing in the platform and large numbers of people and luggage are being discharged as well as quite a lot of mail. 'No wonder she coughed a bit on the way up' says Fred,' there's less joining than leaving so it may be easier once we get out of here - we'll see how she runs'. Now I see why we took water at Pontypool, as this exercise is getting a little drawn out. Fred and the Inspector are looking at watches and swapping war stories of long delays in the blackout around Hereford, and Stan has taken to sweeping up the floorboards and wiping down the water gauge frame and protector and his side of the cab. Fred starts packing his nose warming pipe and has just got it nicely alight when there's much whistling and waving from the rear. The advanced starter signal near our front buffers drops to clear with a loud bang and the station signalman appears at his window with an unfurled green flag. Fred removes his pipe, and pulls the ejector valve handle down to evacuate the brakes. The needles on the duplex gauge start to climb rapidly to 25 inches of vacuum, and he swiftly cracks open the regulator and give her a few forward turns of the reversing screw. As the train brakes come off so she slowly starts to ease the weight of the train ahead and gives several short sharp blasts from the stack, and after travelling a further fifty yards Fred is satisfied she's got all of the train taut behind her and its time to get serious. He winds her quite a way up into forward gear and as the beat sharpens to a lovely deep bass bark he starts to gradually open the regulator wider a bit at a time. 4037's shotgun exhaust starts to blast the sky and passing under a road bridge a lot of it is deflected downward at some pressure. The track curves round to the right up ahead past Brecon Curve box and Fred wants enough momentum to get round without anything binding or sticking.

We blast out past a large goods yard and sidings, and swing onto the curve that takes us round to Barr's Court. There's a large electricity pylon standing in a yard here, being stress tested by the look of the gantries around it. Stan tells me a local firm has the contract for National Grid pylon towers and this is where they are made. That job should keep them going for the next few hundred years. She's pulling well and making a steady 20 as we pass Barr's Court box, which unusually, is sited at the top of a small embankment, with all the rodding and signal wires leading down to the lineside cess below. The box windows are open and the signalman raises a hand as we blast by. Fred and Stan have been shooting the odd look to the rear as well as looking out for the Barr's Court signals and as the track straightens and the train is off the curve, Fred starts to wind her back to a steady roar to ease the pull on the fire and let the water level recover. The exhaust steam injector has been put on with the feed set to a nicely judged stream and the aim, so I'm told, is to work her so that the feed input and steam output balance as far as possible and the demands of the locomotive doesn't run the boiler short of steam. To do this the water level will be kept as steady as possible, allowing for the work in hand. This is second nature to men of their experience, and they know that they will have to work 4037 to her practical limit if time is to be kept.

Chapter 10
An Extended Education

WE LEFT Hereford slightly down due to the double stop - about a minute according to Fred's watch, a venerable but highly accurate H.Samuel pocket watch which belonged to his father, who was also an engineman. It has a nice sterling silver cover to the glass to guard against knocks and scratches, and it lives on the end of a length of heavy sterling silver chain in Fred's overall jacket breast pocket. This was one of four watches we had, but importantly, it was the *drivers* watch, so it's what was used to time the train. I had noticed him check it against the Hereford clock and also earlier at Pontypool, so he must be sure that it's absolutely accurate as he hasn't altered it and after all he is the Driver and outranks everyone here. The Inspector asked his permission for us to board at Bristol, as I recall, and he shot a look at Stan before he nodded. If Stan had grimaced or made a discreet hand movement, it wouldn't have happened and the Inspector would have accepted with good grace. It didn't, I suspect, because Fred had been told at Taunton by the Platform Inspector that he would have guests at Bristol, and since he had a good engine and fireman and was running to time, he was prepared to show them what it was all about. The game changed at Bristol when the extra coach was added, and this upped the ante, but Stan was still willing and so away we went. I only found out this facet of footplate etiquette some years later. In all circumstances, the driver is like the captain of a ship at sea, he is the responsible authority and its his name on the ticket, so he carries the can if things go wrong, presence of an Inspector notwithstanding. In the event of problems along the way the Inspector 'advises and assists', but the driver's name is still the one on the ticket. He has the final say and the final way. I was told this by a former ASLEF branch secretary some years afterwards, and I must say I was treated as a gentleman amongst gentlemen throughout, and never suspected the finer points of protocol. On reflection, it only points up the huge obligations borne by steam age enginemen, with great equanimity as I recall, and very little in the way of aids or labour saving devices to assist them. It was called RESPONSIBILITY and they wore it well. In the event of trouble the buck very definitely stopped there, as there was nowhere else for it to go. It's a pity some of our current masters don't show the same moral strength but I suppose that's progress. Even after 45 years I doff my cap to them.

It struck me that the Russians had put Yuri Gagarin into space a few weeks previously and here I was riding on a machine that would have been immediately recognisable to and appreciated by the great Brunel, who had died 110 years previously. Steam has had a very long reign in Britain.

The line out of Hereford curves around to the north and is on a slight grade. Fred is keeping 4037 hard at it with tremendous stack noise. The workers at a nearby factory, lunching in the sunshine break off a scratch game of football to watch us storm angrily by. Fred says he wants her well up to speed before we hit the draggy rise from Moreton-on-Lugg to Dinmore Tunnel as he wants to give the fire a good pull through to set things up for the rest of the journey. We're non-stop to Salop now, and Fred is starting as he intends to go on. Approaching Shelwick Junction the line from the Malverns, Ledbury and Worcester comes in from the right and running easily round the curve is the fine sight of a well-kept 7904 'Fountains Hall' in lined green livery with a five coach train of BR 'blood and custard' or carmine and cream stock to give it it's official name. The signal box at Shelwick is a squat square brick built one of distinctive style and Fred tells me that between here and Shrewsbury most of them are like that. They look like miniature Herefordshire farmhouses and blend right into their surroundings. Its straight on from here to Moreton-on-Lugg and Fred is not slackening the pace. 7312 and her following train will not even get a sniff of our tail lamp if we carry on like this. 4037 has settled to a loud staccato roar and pressure has returned to just under blowing off point. Stan has set the exhaust injector to taste and is steadily taking his time building up the fire to his liking. He breaks off to catch Moreton distant and home signals and giving Fred the 'All clear', proceeds to wash the footplate down with the 'pep pipe', fed from the injector. Fred has the whistle open at Moreton-on-Lugg for the sake of some farm crossings just beyond the station and we're up to 65 as we hammer through.

Moreton-on-Lugg is a small wayside country station with Army sidings. Hall class 4974 'Talgarth Hall' is standing inside the sidings with a sheeted Army freight ready to leave. The crew are in the cab watching us and the guard is standing on the ground talking to them as we roar through, over the level crossing into open country and up onto a long curved climbing embankment, looking down on fields of steaming crops. It had just rained. Across the countryside there is a large black cloud just beyond Dinmore Hill and its raining very heavily on the other side. It seems incongruous on such a pleasant day, but the air has got noticeably more sultry as we have moved inland, and now and again the thick air must clear. Fred removes his pipe - 'Run up the sail, Stan', but Stan has already anticipated this and is rigging a canvas weather sheet from the cab roof to the front of the tender.

The embankment up to Dinmore is pulling us back and Fred has got the regulator wide open and is easing her out on the screw a notch at a time. Dinmore tunnels are split-level, just like Patchway and the station is split-level as well with platforms on the two separated single lines with gradients of 1 in 135 on our side and 1 in 100 on the other. It's a stiff pull for a 14-coach train but 4037 is lunging on towards the single bore and with firedoors closed and a shriek on the whistle we dive inside. It's a curving climbing bore and Fred is ready to ease her in case of wheelslip on damp rails, but she's hammering confidently on. The sharp performance from Hereford had whitened the fire and the stack was clear as we entered so we're not getting smoke back into the cab even though there's not much clearance between the chimney top and the roof. Unlike the passage of Patchway tunnel, this time we are working all out uphill and on a slight curve. The noise is tremendous in the confined space as the exhaust hits the roof and is bounced down around us as hot breath. The heat on the footplate rises markedly due to the weather sheet, even though the tunnel air must be cool, and on uphill climbs in a tight bore like this there must be a risk of crews being overcome by heat or fumes especially if the engine enters with a heavy smoky fire. The Inspector tells me there is, which is why they are careful in the way the fire is managed and also it is not that long a tunnel. Ledbury and Colwall tunnels on the Worcester line are similarly tight and with heavy trains and doubtful engines a prudent crew sometimes request an assisting engine, as nobody wants to stall in a rathole like this with a heavy train.

Coming round the bend we can see daylight ahead but it looks very grey and as we get closer we can see that its torrential rain. Diving out into this, its time to keep the head inside. Warm rain hitting a hot loco gives us a sudden curtain of steam all over which is soon dissipated by our slipstream and looking up the rain is actually being deflected horizontally over our heads and very little is falling onto us. The hot smokebox is causing a small cloud of vapoury steam to proceed before us and a torrent of water is running down through the coal in the tender and vanishing under the fall plate into the gap between it and the engine. Before I have time to take it all in we're out of the squall as quickly as we had entered it. Stan is busy, washing down with the pep pipe and brushing slurry away, with a final wash clean of the floorboards ready for further work. In a few quick moves he furls the weather sheet and stows it back up under the cab roof. Stan is never idle, what with shovel, handbrush and looking out for signals or anything untoward. It could be an act for the Inspector's sake, but I think not. After watching him for a while I realise that he is working in concert with his mate, and is anticipating his actions and setting of the controls in an almost clairvoyant fashion. He has in fact fallen into, and is working with the rhythm of the machine and the methods of the driver. Yet not a word passes between them, each man being intent on his own task, but each knows what the other is doing. The Inspector notices that I have noticed, and tells me that the old hands know exactly what they are doing, and with their respective knowledge of road, engine and train working, no word needs to pass between them in periods of great concentration. Conversation is almost impossible anyway because of the noise and vibration, so communication is by shout, sign language, whistles or gestures. I can only speak to the Inspector very close up, Fred and Stan communicate by nod, wink and hand signals, depending on where we are and what appears to be happening. It's a steady climb apart from some respite, all the way to Church Stretton and both are working steadily to ensure that we get there and over the top in good time.

Ford Bridge signals are off for a clear run through and the signalman in the small brick box by the crossing raises a hand as we pass. 4037 is roaring away in fine style. Stan is firing steadily round the box, keeping just in front of the need for hot plentiful steam. Fourteen coaches should be enough to wind any 'Castle' on an uphill stretch but the Inspector explained a technique known as 'mortgaging the boiler' which was used when overloaded on steep grades. It took some doing and even the older hands had to plan carefully, but it allowed a steam locomotive to be worked well beyond its normal maximum steaming rate for short periods of time, which is a characteristic that steam locomotives have. I was about to see a great demonstration of this technique and its something I have never seen described before in any railway book.

Fred removed his pipe and spoke a few words to the Inspector which I didn't catch, then knocked the bowl of his pipe out against the cabside, and wrapping it in cotton waste, for it was a well burned in briar, put it in his pocket. He beckoned me over to his side and told me I was to see the job from the other side. At that Stan slid the shovel neatly back under some choice lumps and stepped across to stand behind me, Fred picked up the shovel and started to steadily fire where Stan left off. I think they all saw the look on my face and were highly amused. Stan told me he and Fred always change over at some point, and at Taunton Fred had told Stan he would fire from Dinmore to Church Stretton to give Stan a spell, and since Stan was a driver anyway, Fred had no qualms about doing it. Stan wasn't just a fireman, he was a trusted mate and Fred had earlier fired from Exeter to Whiteball on this journey, taking over the driving again as the train had reached the summit of the climb out of Devon at Whiteball Box. On a job like this, Stan told me they would swap over at least once during the trip as Fred held that since Stan was a driver 'he'd better do some driving before he loses his touch'. Our Inspector didn't turn a hair, as he said he had often done the same when a driver with his firemen, especially when they were going before the Inspector for their driver's exam. The difference was that I was going to drive her for a short while under Stan's and the Inspector's tutelage while Fred fired, just, as they said 'to get the feel of her'. Picking up a handful of cotton waste from the ball of it in the fireman's bucket he passes me some and tells me to make a pad of it in my palm, as it'll make using the controls easier. Fred had always used a wad of cotton waste in his hand while driving 4037, both as a pad and to wipe his hands on. I only ever saw this stuff used on the footplate and have never seen it anywhere else. I would have thought an industrial wiping rag would have been better, but Western men prefer cotton waste, which looks like coarse multi coloured cotton wool. It's very soft and absorbent and good for wiping up spilt oil and cleaning down generally. It also stops any hot fittings from burning the hands, although everything on the boiler face is hot and small burns and singes are sometimes taken in their stride as part of the job. A lot of the steam valve handles have hardwood ferrules which makes them less likely to burn, but the regulator handle and reverser are polished fine grain steel which can leave a nice blister unless cushioned by something in the palm. Compared to some industrial jobs the footplate is no more dangerous than many others and by the time men graduate to this sort of work they have been brought up in a very hard school and know exactly what they are doing. I would be very surprised if either of them had suffered so much as a blister for years past.

Chapter 11
The Mortgage Men

FRED oiled the firedoor slides, opened the doors wide and set the dampers to his liking. Since we were in for about an hour of all out effort, he told me that he would shovel steadily all the way from here to Church Stretton, while Stan drove, and would build up a 'lime burner' or 'hogs back' fire to act as a store of heat to be drawn upon during the climb. This would thoroughly warm up the refractory brick arch in the firebox about three feet above the grate and stretching back for about two thirds of its length. This served to promote efficient combustion by lengthening the gas path, reflecting heat back onto the firebed and acting as an additional reservoir of heat. This was a necessary adjunct to the mortgaging exercise along with an exhaust steam injector which worked cleanly over its entire range, allowing water to be trickled or flooded into the boiler as needs dictate. We were non-stop to Shrewsbury so the regulator went right up against the stop - fully open - and stayed there, with the counterweight stopping it from shaking shut. The working of the engine was now to be controlled by the use of the cut-off or reverse screw, known to Western men as 'working her on the lever'. Fred was sweeping up after each round of firing and putting the small coal and dust straight into the firebox. Small coal underfoot is a safety hazard, so any spillage was quickly removed. No wonder both of them were built like prize-winning whippets. Once they got into the rhythm they just didn't stand still. Like Stan, Fred was looking out for signals that may be hard to see from the driver's side, and of course he knew where every one was, and giving Stan the nod as he saw them at clear. We hadn't had a signal check since the cows on the line at Tram Inn, so efficient regulation between signalmen and Control must be taking place. Every one of them had seen the size of our train, and realised the difficulties inherent in a restart in an awkward place and the knock on effect on following traffic.

Stan told me that from here on, the engine was to be worked to keep the water level at between two-thirds and three-quarters of a glass with the level only being allowed to drop to half a glass or under during the final few miles from Craven Arms to Church Stretton summit, which is actually at Little Stretton Halt. The injector had been set to feed water steadily according to Fred's judgement, and Stan would work the engine by constantly adjusting the cut-off to compensate for changes in gradient and try and keep the rate of steam flow to the cylinders as constant as possible with no sudden demands that would take her 'off the boil'. It is all done with Stan keeping one eye on the water gauge and listening to her beat, and trying to keep speed constant, while letting Fred worry about the pressure. All this and signals and train running too - nothing to do with steam locomotives was achieved without substantial mental and physical effort. With a fourteen-coach train, there was absolutely no margin for error and it all had to be very finely judged. With a ten or twelve coach train, which Fred called 'a boys train', there would have been something in hand, but with fourteen coaches over this road it was a case of maximum effort over a long period just to maintain the point to point timings, which would have been eased a little due to the exceptional load. No words passed between them about this, both men knew exactly what had to be done and just got on with it. As an example of quiet professionalism in any field I have never seen it equalled since.

Pressure was between 215 and 220 and Fred told me that he wanted to hold her at just below blowing off point at 222/223, and I didn't doubt for a moment that he would be able to do it. He looked to me like a man bent on serious business. At that pressure she would just be lifting the safety valve, or 'showing a blossom' as they said, effectively balanced at full pressure but with no wasteful blowing off. Blowing off wasted about a gallon of water a minute anyway, and with the way we were going through the stuff we didn't want to waste any and have to worry about it - a good fill on Bromfield troughs should see us right.

Fred's father was an enginemen, and he spent fifteen years firing before he became a driver, to some old boys who really knew the job and passed something on. He still fires now from time to time and with the right mate, as he regards it as a more skilful job than driving and as he says, it keeps his head and his arteries clear. It's a slight, draggy climb from Ford Bridge to Leominster through gorgeous open countryside and I'm told to link her up until she feels right. It's down to me, they say, I'm the driver, the three of them looking at me like the three wise monkeys. They all see the look on my face and tell me to get on with it. Stan tells me to give her a bit more so I wind the screw forward to 45%. 4037 starts to chatter stridently at the stack, with the exhaust arching well up over the train. Fred pulls up the firehole flap to leave a small quadrant open to the air. The air is whistling through the gap to feed the seething white mass, which now hurts the eyes to look at. Putting the shovel down he empties the contents of the Hereford station fire bucket into it. A Great Western shovel is large enough to take a half-hundredweight of coal if necessary, so a bucket full of sand fills it neatly to the rim. The Inspector makes a point of intently studying the lineside fields of corn while Fred gently feeds the whole shovelful of sand over the firedoor flap by lifting the shovel while the blade is balanced on the edge of the flap. The sand is drawn from the shovel into the firebox and the suction down the tubes accelerates it to supersonic speeds before it gets blasted high up out of the stack by the exhaust. We emit a rather large cloud of black smoke, which soon clears behind us. 'That's cleared her throat ' says Fred. Any soot that may have formed or be about to form on the tubes has now been cleared by this impromptu sand blasting exercise. He tells me this sort of trick is not done unless necessary and then only in open country, and preferably with no Inspector about, but with fourteen on and Church Stretton bank ahead this is no time for the squeamish, and that's why they wanted me to 'give her the whip' as they put it. We have surged angrily forward and Stan tells me to wind her back until 'she's purring along'. I wind the screw back to 35%, and he says 'a bit more' and at 30%, 'leave her at that for now'. He's right, she's purring along like a well-fed tigress and is really hitting her stride.

I'm standing braced against the gentle roll of 4037, with one hand on the reverser and the other resting on the brake handle, looking straight ahead down the length of the boiler and running plate at the track unfolding ahead. 4037 is pulling hard and apart from the vibration and stack noise is riding steadily and well. There is no pitching, lurching or banging, and Stan is behind me where he can sight signals and give instructions directly into my ear. Fred is whistling to himself and intently firing to a clear stack and white-hot fire and the Inspector is sitting on the fireman's seat jotting on his clipboard, breaking now and then to look ahead or behind. Everyone is fully occupied and I feel that I more than have my hands full.

Stan is talking conversationally into my ear, telling me what to look for and why. He says they do this exercise whenever they have a management trainee travelling with them. The railways are taking on graduates as putative managers under a training scheme, and apparently its not unusual these days to come across one travelling around with a footplate pass, sent out to gain motive power experience. Some crews tell them to stand in the corner and shut up, but ours tend to make them work their passage, as Fred holds that a manager is no good unless he knows, and has experienced what the men have to do, so at some point a coal splitting, firing and driving exercise is arranged and if they don't end the day with a few blisters and an aching back then they haven't learned anything or had their money's worth as far as this crew are concerned. In their view it may also be the first honest day's sweat some of these characters have ever put in, so that adds both to its educational and entertainment value. I'm beginning to see what they mean.

We're approaching Leominster and with the distant signal off and the ATC bell ringing in my ear, it looks like a clear run through. Leominster was a large junction at one time but the branches to Kington and Presteigne were closed to passengers in the 1951 coal crisis, as well as the Worcester line as far as Bromyard, so it's not as busy as it once was, but its still quite important. We're not booked to stop here, as the following connecting train from Hereford will decant our West Country passengers so we must make as much speed as possible to pick up any running time we might lose on the steeper stretches. Its slightly upgrade (1 in 408), followed by level, followed by a slight upgrade (1 in 460), followed by another level stretch. The levels should allow us to recover from any slowing on the grades, unless we have sufficient momentum to 'flatten the hump' as Stan says. We're up to 60 after a good deal of slogging helped by the short downgrade from Ford Bridge and 4037 is thoroughly warmed through and has really got hold of the train. The sun is setting her shadow in sharp relief on the opposite track and I can see the exhaust and the blossom from the safety valve and my own shadow showing against the blurred sleepers of the down line. Approaching the sidings at the south end two freights behind their respective War Department (WD) 2-8-0's are standing in the up and down loop sidings, and it looks like a change of crews is taking place. Stan tells me to link her up a little more, to 25%, and to give a long blast on the whistle. He says to be sure to use the nearer lower whistle chain and not the other one, as that is the emergency whistle, with a quite different tone. If railwaymen hear that then they are all 'on the jump' as it means something is going wrong. If the guard in the van hears it blowing loud and long he'll lift his brake setter and attempt to stop the train, as he might think we have been overcome by some emergency. It's a good job he told me so I'll keep my fingers well away from it.

The men in the distance, about to cross the track, see and hear us and raise an arm in acknowledgement, and stand well clear of the running lines, as the Rule Book suggests. The goods yard here is very busy, with a 1400 class tank shunting quietly. The south end signalman raises a dustered hand in acknowledgement and can be seen looking back down our train as we pass through. He is looking to see that we are correct and complete and carrying a tail lamp, with no non-horizontal door handles, smoke or haze from axleboxes or anything else that may prompt a 'Stop and Examine' code to Leominster Station box.

From the driver's side I see an LMR 'Royal Scot' rushing towards us with a southbound express, 46126 trailing 11 coaches which pass with a roar and tremendous slipstream. Whistling again for the station, and running under clear signals, passengers waiting on the platform take a few steps back, as we bear down on them at nearly 70 with whistle screaming. The signal box at Leominster Station is up on a gantry over the island platform and the signalman above raises a hand as we pass and is looking intently back down our train. Just north of the station is a level crossing which was shut to let the 'Royal Scot' and its southbound train through, it's still shut and there's a long queue of cars and lorries on either side. Some car drivers have got out to see what the noise is about, and as we plummet through with shrieking whistle and strident chattering exhaust many, both male and female, look on with undisguised awe at the sheer theatricality of our passage. Wherever you are in this country, the passage of a fast moving steam express train always causes people to pause and look. One man is holding his small son up in his arms and following our progress, and many wave to us as we roar past over the crossing with our lengthy train in tow.

The next place to look out for is the signalbox at Berrington, actually at the now closed station of Berrington and Eye, which sits between two small villages. Near the line is the large white Palladian mansion of Berrington Hall and all hands are anxious that I see it, as an especially good view can be had from the footplate. We're on the level here and speed is rising steadily, followed by a short upgrade which I can see ahead, but with our speed and the momentum of the train behind us we surmount it easily, onto the next stretch of level track beyond. I see what they meant about a series of steps all the way to Church Stretton. There's a short sharp upgrade at the end of this stretch and we can see Berrington and Eye. Whistling through the slight curve at Berrington, we pass an intent signalman watching us closely. The windows and the door to the box are open on this warm day and a Labrador dog is dozing on the threshold. The signalman's dog hardly moves his head as we hurtle by under clear signals- it's just another train - so what? It's a bit of a sawtooth profile from here to Woofferton Junction with two sharp little hills approached by 1 in 150 and 1 in 100 gradients. The only good thing is that they have corresponding downgrades so what we lose on the up we gain on the down.

Chapter 12
Rural Theatre

THEY tell me to give her 35% on the upgrades, which makes her shout at the stack, and wind her back to 25% on the downgrades which settles her to a deep purr. The water level is changing with the grades as they have said, but pressure is holding steady in a range between 220 and 225. I find this amazing given the treatment 4037 is getting, but to these two everything is running exactly as planned.

Fred is looking out for Woofferton distant signal and seeing it clear he gives us a hand signal. The ATC bell goes off in my ear as we pass it and Stan reaches over to cancel it. We're on the 1 in 100 downgrade into Woofferton and as the remainder of the train passes onto the downgrade speed is rapidly rising. Given that we had maintained a steady 55-65 since Leominster then it rapidly rises to 75 and 4037 really comes into her own. Rolling and lurching gently, she's rushing forward down the grade and Stan tells me to give a long, long blast on the whistle right up to the platform end to warn the unwary to stand well back. We start whistling well out and by the time Woofferton comes into sight there seem to be a lot of people on the platform but standing well back from the edge. He tells me to 'sharpen her stack a little' and giving her two notches on the screw her note deepens slightly, and to keep the whistle open. The crowd is starting to flatten against the fencing and buildings and we can see station staff ushering them well back. Its downhill into Woofferton and we're now doing 85 with a wide open whistle and running in front of a very heavy train. Passing down the platforms there a lot of awestruck faces looking our way. A lot of the men have a slight appreciative half smile, but many of the women are looking very apprehensive. A small girl with a doll clutched tightly to her is turning half in to her mothers skirt almost in fear but with both eyes fixed on the hurtling behemoth. Our eyes meet as I smile and wave at her and her face brightens a little, all done in a split second, and she vanishes behind. There's a cloud of ballast dust, straw and paper shards rising behind us and some turn away from it as our slipstream between the platforms is quite strong.

I catch a glimpse of an Ivatt 2-6-2 tank, 41204 standing in the bay platform with three coaches, ready for the cross-country run through Tenbury Wells and Newnham Bridge to Kidderminster and across the fields is a very mysterious radar base which nobody is anxious to talk about. There's a very large signal box on the right near the junction for the Tenbury line and the signalman plus what looks like a signalling inspector are watching us. Still shrieking on the whistle I raise a hand in acknowledgement and with Stan speaking in my ear 'All off, keep her going' we rush through into the open countryside south of Ludlow, exhaust roaring from the stack and a blossom at the safety valves. The pressure gauge is just steady at 224/225, and Fred is as good as his word. As she starts to rasp at the stack Stan tells me to 'drop her back two notches' and then 'OK I'll have her back now', and we swap places with me now standing behind him. The Inspector is jotting in his journal and Fred is looking out for Ludlow distant signal. The track ahead is climbing towards Ludlow in a series of steps and at any one time we could be on three different gradients given the length of our train. The tremendous momentum from our descent into Woofferton is propelling us along and all we have to do as Stan says 'is stay out of the train's way' We climb quickly towards Ludlow in fine style, and Fred catches the Ludlow distant signal from a way off and having seen that at clear and letting Stan know by a loud whistle and a hand signal, he throws two good shovelfuls onto the seething mass and shuts the firehole doors.

Ludlow Tunnel is up ahead and he wants to avoid a blowback. He confirms the outer home signal at clear as we get closer and then turns to pull some good coal forward and break up a few large lumps at the shovel plate. Passing the back gardens of the outskirts of Ludlow, there are several people mowing lawns and lazing in deckchairs and one family appear to be engaged in painting a garden fence en masse, which as Fred says is one way to share the pain on a hot day. I'm feeling a little sticky with my overalls on over my clothes and I will have to change at Shrewsbury as I can feel sweat running down my back. It's pleasantly breezy on the footplate, but I can see why so much tea is drunk. Without it sheer dehydration would soon set in and in hot conditions, tea either hot or cold quenches thirst better than water. Whistling shrilly, we race through the short Ludlow Tunnel, through the station with bystanders standing well back from the edge, and on to the long S-bend passing 5322 shunting the pick up freight in Ludlow up goods yard, heeling first right and then left as we pass round the long curve, our massive train following smoothly and sinuously behind in good order. 4037 rides round it like a limousine with hardly a snatch or lurch and runs steadily on. We appear to have hit the spot with all steam locomotives where they run, ride and steam to best advantage and 4037 is shaping up well for the climb ahead.

Acknowledging the hand signal from Ludlow box, urging us on, Fred opens the firedoors and starts steadily building up the fire again. The regulator is still wide open with 30% cut-off and with pressure steady at just below blowing off, she's packing plenty of punch and working hard. Fred tinkers a little with the exhaust injector to adjust the feed, and Stan continues to keep one eye on the water level and the other strictly on the road ahead. The fire is built up in a solid white hot wedge from half way up the firehole door aperture and is mounded forward under the brick arch, and it must be doing its job as the steam pressure has hardly faltered from just under 225 and as far as I can see 4037 is being fairly leathered along with no visible or aural ill effect. I realise that Fred is not looking at where he is putting his shovel shots. He's putting it in on the basis of instinct and experience it seems, and he's obviously working to a tried and trusted formula. He certainly appears to know exactly where we are at any time as he will break off and sight signals that may be difficult to see from the driver's side, before resuming his rhythmic pattern of work.

Coming off the curve there's a straight stretch up past Ludlow Racecourse, which is on the right hand side. Bromfield distant is off so we can approach at full speed. Bromfield troughs are just beyond, and passing Bromfield level crossing and box Fred crosses to the scoop handle and begins to wind it down. He's watching the water gauge and slowly counting seconds away. As soon as he winds down he begins to wind it back up. The water gauge has climbed to nearly 4000 gallons so there'll be more than enough to take us to Shrewsbury, even at the rate we're drinking the stuff. Bromfield is a tricky trough they tell me as there is an accommodation crossing just beyond and if you are slow getting the scoop up, you'll lose the end of it, which is made of lead, on the boards of the crossing. Fred reckons a local farmer has put a fine roof on a piggery using flattened out scoop ends that were removed by this crossing over the years. This may be one of Fred's tall tales but given his deadpan delivery and gravitas, one does wonder. Frank Lewis looked on with a twinkle in his eye and said nothing.

That's it. The last piece of the plan is in place. No worries about water now, so battle can be joined. The atmosphere changed on the footplate, this was where the deadly serious business of the day finally gets done. The Inspector pulled a few large lumps down with the coal pick and deftly split them along the grain, and poking around, pulled a few more likely lumps within range. The tip up seats were secured up out of the way and using the 'pep pipe' Fred washed down the floorboards sending dust and loose small coal over the side. The fire has been built up to a mound just over halfway up the firehole door space and with the dampers full open and the firedoors wide open Fred can regulate the flow of secondary or top air onto the fire by adding more coal in the right places. He's now using the supply of coal to control combustion, which may sound obvious, but is a carefully managed state of affairs. Even though the firedoors are open wide, the mound of coal at the firedoor entrance is both warming and regulating the secondary air as well as allowing freshly added coal to get fully alight before the considerable blast from the stack draws it toward the front of the firebox as it gets burnt down to a smaller size.

The hills are closing in around us and off to the right is Clee Hill and in the distance Wenlock Edge, a beautiful smudgy grey-blue under this summer sky. Closing in to the left are the hills of the Clun Forest and we're making our way along the valley of the River Onny towards Onibury. A 'Grange' class engine, 6836 'Estevarney Grange', approaches on the other track heading a long string of vans and passes with a clattering roar The main Shrewsbury road comes into sight on the left and we are passing the heavier traffic as we are roaring along at a steady 55 which is excellent going on this slight upgrade- 1 in 870 - with the load we're pulling. Some saloon and sports cars are leaving us behind, and one or two are pacing us with the occupants looking and listening to us working at almost full stretch. I say almost, because as the gradient steepened slightly, Stan gave her another few notches and she immediately sharpened her beat, and I could feel her surge forward, like a racehorse on the home stretch. Fred is slowly and steadily adding half-shovelfuls in just the right places, and pauses to adjust the exhaust injector to feed slightly more as the water level was starting to drop down. She's dropped pressure a few pounds, but by pulling up the flap plate and dropping a few large lumps to sit just inside the firehole, he restricts the cold secondary air slightly and the pressure stabilises at 220 - this is fine artistry of a high order and Frank Lewis is busily jotting in his journal and whistling quietly to himself - nothing for him to worry about on this trip, it seems. Looking back down the train there's a head at every window and droplight it seems and many are enjoying the scenery, as this part of Shropshire is quite beautiful. This must be a prize length as 4037 is riding very well with no bangs or lurches and pulling very hard. The noise from the stack is tremendous and I don't think we'll need a whistle as our exhaust is thrown back loudly from lineside buildings and bridges. No wonder there's a head at every window - they must wonder just what is going on. We're on a curving stretch and Stan gives her another two notches to bring her up to 40% cut off to counteract the binding effect of fourteen coaches leaning on the lower rail of a curve and 4037 is really playing stack music. Fred is putting cobs of coal on the mound just inside the door at steady intervals. He's taking his time and choosing his lumps at the shovel plate, and as they land just inside the door they appear to almost explode into combustion in the intense white heat of the firebox. It's the trapped gas in the Welsh coal says Fred. If coal is left stacked for too long it goes off, he says which is why you can have 'good' tenderfuls of coal and 'bad' tenderfuls depending on where the coal was dug and how long its been in wagons, coal stages or tenders before being used. This stuff is quite good, large lumps with a good grain which reflects the light and darkly black with no tinge of grey which would denote weathering or a long time in the stack. Some of the coal is NCB ovoid briquettes that are marketed by the Coal Board as locomotive fuel, but can be of doubtful quality. Fred is avoiding this stuff, as with plenty of good Welsh in easy reach he doesn't have to use it. ('We'll only burn those after we've burnt the cab seats', was his comment)

He's built a glorious deep fire in her, and since 'Castles' were designed to burn best Welsh she's doing what she was designed to do in fine style. I comment on the hard running with this train and Fred tells me they used to run trains this big all the time before and during the War, but he says coal and maintenance were better, especially before the War, and you nearly always had good engines on a job like this. We're lucky today because 4037 is a good low-mileage one only a few months out of the shops and they spent time at Newton this morning checking her and ensuring smokebox and ashpan were as clean as possible before starting. As long as all the basics are right and with good coal a trip like this is tolerable but if anything goes wrong with running or performance then you can be in trouble for both steam and time. The climb has sharpened slightly as we approach Onibury but we're still making a good pace at about 50, and Onibury's signals are all clear and the crossing gates are shut and locked against quite a queue of road traffic. Once again watchers are gathering at the crossing and the Onibury signalman steps into the box doorway for an unimpeded view. Whistling shrilly, we slam over the crossing, urging our huge train on and over the bridge over the Onny at which point the gradient sharpens. We've built a fair momentum but the weight of the train is just starting to drag as Stan starts easing out on the cut off, a notch at a time, watching the road ahead, pressure gauge, water gauge and signals as he does so. Fred is busy adjusting the dampers and exhaust injector feed and pressure is steady at about 222. They both have the absolute measure of the job and the machine and as there's a small hill up to Craven Arms they want to maintain as much speed and punch as they can. On up the valley we can see Stokesay Castle to the right, one of the finest examples of a fortified manor house on the Welsh borders and close to the accommodation crossing we are met by 70021 'Morning Star' roaring south at the head of a packed twelve coach express, which gives a long howl on its three-chime American whistle as it hurtles by . Still making a steady 50 we climb over the hump just south of Craven Arms and with the Craven Arms signals showing clear it's whistle time again.

Chapter 13
Craven Arms

CRAVEN ARMS is the junction for the Central Wales line which is the ex-LMS route to Swansea. The line is single track over its upland stretches and carries a large amount of long distance freight traffic to Swansea Docks, West Wales and Fishguard. In the summer it becomes busier due to the pressure on the coastal and other North - South routes as well as the passenger service between Shrewsbury and Swansea. It's quite a busy line and Craven Arms is it's northern end. It offers an alternative route to Swansea and the discerning traveller can sometimes change from a Manchester - Swansea express at Craven Arms and taking the alternative route, get to Swansea slightly quicker than the so-called direct train. It's a downgrade in the northbound direction through Craven Arms and once again it's a matter of gaining as much momentum as possible for the climb ahead to Little Stretton. We're gaining speed as the whole fourteen coaches come over the hump, and on the left is the Central Wales Line junction with its sharply curved connection. There's a class 8F 2-8-0 standing at signals with a train of oil tanks, from Milford Haven I'm told, obviously waiting for us to pass, and the signalman at Craven Arms South gives us the 'all clear' handsignal as we sweep past him under clear signals. With whistle wide open to warn the unwary we descend upon Craven Arms and lurching slightly over the junction pointwork, 4037 straightens up and continues the pell-mell pace. A Central Wales line train headed by BR Standard 5 73092 is standing at the other side of the island platform and a few yards in front of it is another 8F waiting to leave as a light engine as soon as we pass. This is not lost on our Inspector. 'They must have held the Swansea train for us to pass, and the light engine will follow us at a respectable distance, to assist if we get stuck on the hill'. Given his knowledge and the use he has been making of the working timetable in the last half-hour I'm quite prepared to believe him. It would make good sense, and it has been apparent, even from my viewpoint that Control have been smoothing our way northward as much as possible. There's a glimpse of Craven Arms shed with three 8F's and a Fowler 2-6-4 tank simmering in the sunshine and with a lurch and a momentary flash of upturned faces we pass over Craven Arms Crossing and onto the main climb with a vengeance. They worked her up to 60 during the short switchback descent, and we must have made an awesome sight passing through Craven Arms with a clear, high exhaust and dust and papers swirling in our wake. It's a steady slog over 1 in 100 ruling grades with only two short respites, from here to just past Marsh Farm Junction, followed by a short downhill and then uphill at 1 in 112 after Marshbrook all the way to the summit at Little Stretton. This is where the all out effort must take place and what all the scheme and toil from Hereford has been about. She's showing a three quarter full glass and pressure just below 225, with a sharp exhaust and a clear stack which only darkens very slightly as Fred lobs a few choice lumps in to fill the right spots in his colossal mass of a fire. With the firehole flap down 'to give her enough air to breath properly' as he puts it, Fred stops to fish out his pipe, puts a plug of tobacco in and using a large brass trench lighter, lights up and sits down on the fireman's seat. 'She's as full as an egg' he says' that should see us to the top and its all downhill and keeping her quiet from there on'. The heat from the fire is such that I cannot stand in line with it, as my overalls start to singe, so I'm standing behind Stan as he's tuning her with the reverse screw to counteract every nuance of gradient and curvature. This is being done by feel and experience. From the sound at the stack and the kick, or absence of it, in the trailing axleboxes beneath our feet Stan can feel how happy she is with the load and the gradient. In these dry conditions she's unlikely to slip except where we pass a leafy stretch through the trees a bit further on. Fallen leaves and moisture give an excellent lubricant under the weight of an engine and she might slip if we're not careful.

It's a sharpening curving climb from here to Little Stretton, about six miles up the valley, and we are starting, as calculated, in very good order with a full box of live white fire, about three quarters of a glass of water which should allow for adequate superheating without water being carried over, a clear stack and a sharp whiplash exhaust. Stan is watching the road ahead intently, not so much looking for signals, he tells me but curvature. Momentum has to be kept up on climbing curving stretches with a long heavy train as if the train is strung out round a reverse curve such as we have here, the flange resistance and weight can sometimes cause a train to stall if there is not enough rolling momentum to overcome it. The trick is to keep the whole circus rolling along under slightly positive acceleration as far as possible, and this is where the boiler mortgaging exercise comes in. For a short period, we are going to work 4037 beyond her normal limits, to get over this difficult stretch. This can be done from time to time with a steam locomotive, given the thermal reservoir that exists in the heat contained in boiler, firebox and brick arch. But it's a one shot affair, do it too early or too much and you'll be stuck short of steam and stall on the gradient. If that happens we'll be glad of that 8F shuffling along light one block behind us. But if it's done right, as seems about to be demonstrated, then we will clamber to the top in good order and keeping reasonable time. Fred explained that we were automatically allowed extra running time from Bristol as a result of the load being increased. We are on the absolute limit for an unassisted 'Castle' over this road and we have done very well to keep reasonably to time. He reckoned we were a minute and a half adrift of where we should have been, but given the point to point times allowed for the road and the increased load we were about right. The working timetable says we should have been through here about two minutes ago, and he would like to hand over the train to the London Midland Region at Shrewsbury 'right time' if possible. The only way that will get done is a strident climb to Stretton followed by a fast descent all the way to Sutton Bridge Junction at the bottom of the hill.

Stan has the regulator right up against the stop, and since he knows she is carrying full boiler pressure due to Fred's work, he is regulating her working and steam consumption by advancing the cut off to the point where the hydrostatic lubricator is feeding about three to four good drops a minute. He can tell from this how the engine is taking steam at the steam chest, since it's the pressure differential between boiler and steam chest that allows it to work, and given the note from the stack he knows how well she is pacing herself. It's all done by sound and feel, through the ears and the soles of the feet. The front end is getting a good oiling also, and by working her at a steady steam consumption rate using these little tricks of the trade, 4037 can be extended to full stretch and should be able to go over the top at All Stretton without too much trouble. Frank Lewis is looking out at the countryside and talking to Fred, who, pipe in mouth is contemplating the road ahead. Stan is 'working her on the lever' as they say, advancing the reverser forward or back a notch or two to keep her speed and steam consumption steady on the changing grades which run 1 in 130, 1 in 105, 1 in 268, a bit of level then more of the same. This length of train can not only be on two differing gradients, but on a set of curves at the same time so plenty of punch at the crank and a steady steam rate is required. We're lucky it's a dry day and we don't have to use sand. Fred tells me he's had a train stall, and have to be assisted away before now, on a dirty day with high winds and dragging an overload like this. In circumstances like that he has been known to stop at Craven Arms for an assisting engine having wired ahead from Hereford. Sometimes Control have already arranged it. This comes down to local knowledge and how closely signalmen watch our progress northwards and report back. On some occasions he has wrapped a note round a small piece of coal and lobbed it out at a signalbox. Desperate times breed desperate measures he says. Obviously we have done well enough on the way up for somebody to judge that we will not have too many problems getting there, but the ambling 8F behind us is there as discreet insurance, plus it probably had to go to Shrewsbury anyway.

Speed has dropped to 30 on the 1 in 130 up to Wistanstow, but she shows no sign of labouring and steam pressure is being maintained and so is water level. Fred has got the exhaust injector set very finely and on the steeper stretches she loses water level and on the slighter stretches it steadies. She's being held at just under two thirds of a glass so some has been lost. Frank Lewis tells me the working range on the glass is about two and a half inches meaning you allow the level to fluctuate to the minimum but by no more than two and a half inches on a climb like this, as that represents the capacity to be expended before the boiler is sufficiently cooled to lead to a shortage of steam. The exhaust injector is absolutely indispensable. It can be set very finely to feed hot water to match the steam consumption rate, which means that even under heavy working the water level should remain steady. On the home stretch to the summit with the end in sight, Stan will deliberately extend her so as to draw on the reservoir of hot steam and water and over-extend her to the extent that the water level will fall the two and a half inches in the glass but be no more than just under half full as she dips her nose at Little Stretton Summit. This is what mortgaging the boiler means, as once over the top we won't need the steam, so the boiler can be refilled on the descent to Shrewsbury...and all of this to be done without allowing wasteful blowing off.

I'm watching coal dust dancing on the floorboards to the sound from the stack, and we are forging up the valley into a narrowing gorge, then onto a short level, then on up to Marsh Farm Box where the Much Wenlock branch used to depart, closed since 1951.

Up at 1 in 130 then over a hump and down before back up again to hit a sharp curving stretch in the narrow valley up to Marshbrook. This is where 4037 is really showing her breeding. We're climbing steadily away on the sharp curves and looking down the train there's a head at almost every window, and it can't be just for the sunshine. She must look a fine sight and sound working this hard against the grade and perhaps some watchers realise that you won't see stuff like this for that much longer. That's why I'm here and I'm now glad I came.

Marshbrook is everything a country station should be, with a square brick signal box, a small goods yard, level crossing, stone buildings and a pub just over the road, nice and handy. Coming uphill we can see Marshbook distant off and also the home signals around the curve. She's doing a steady 35-40 on a dry rail and making a loud steady pace. We are all standing against the sides of the cab to keep away from the heat, and Fred, puffing on his pipe pauses to leisurely drop a few choice large lumps in just at the back of the firebox, and then sits back down. Passing Marshbrook the beer garden and benches outside the pub are doing good business from the carriage trade judging by the number of parked cars, and as we pass Fred leans out waves and gives a code on the whistle. One of the seated drinkers lifts his pint, waves and is obviously laughing. Its Fred's usual fireman, who is on a rest day as he's temporarily a driver. Fred spotted him and he spotted Fred at the same instant, hence the laughter. Still, we were hammering by with a clear stack, a full pot, Fred sitting down with his pipe going, showing a blossom at the safety valves and pulling fourteen packed coaches at a respectable pace on the curving 1 in 112. There were many rapt watchers, as they must have heard us approaching all the way from Craven Arms, and good many were standing and sitting outside in the sunshine. Fred reckons it will give them food for thought, and show him that the old boys can still do the job. He'll hear more about this in the messroom in a few days time. The watcher will probably comment on the crowd on the footplate and ask Fred why he needed so much help, is he that far past it, or some such comment. There's some badinage yet to be had he reckons.

We're on the sinuous final stretch to Little Stretton and now we can extend her. Stan gives her a notch at a time and the exhaust note gets a little deeper and sharper and she starts to give a little kick at the rear end. As this effect eases off, he gives her a notch more, and then keeps his eye on the water level. She's noticeably surged a little and now settles to the final part of the climb. From the confident beat at the stack, there no hint of overload or hesitation and she's biting into the dry rail and rolling the huge train steadily upward. An LMS class 5, 45290 gives a whoop on its hooter and passes by on the other track with a four coach Swansea train as we pass the landmark of Ragleth Hill on the right hand side. The valley is quite narrow here before opening up on the final stretch to Church Stretton. The Long Mynd is on the left-hand side and away around the curve is Little Stretton Halt, where all our troubles are over. Stan decides to give her a bit more as the end is in sight and and her beat changes to an angry whiplash crack which echoes across the valley. The water level starts slowly to move, but steam pressure is staying constant at 223. 'If I put a teaspoonful more on she'll blow off' says Fred, and I believe him. 4037 is being worked to the maximum, as there's only about five hundred yards to go to Little Stretton Halt. Our exhaust is going straight up for about thirty feet in the air before falling back, and its very light grey in colour, as Fred is literally picking up and dropping lumps of coal in just where he wants them, standing back and lobbing them in like a careful bowls player, into the seething mass within the firebox. 4037 is making and using steam at a prodigious rate given her modest size, and I get a strong impression of every rivet, seam and component being stressed to the limit. Speed has fallen to 23 at which she has a heavy deliberate beat but she's still pulling strongly. Stan says 'that's enough' and as we pass the short platforms of Little Stretton Halt she gains a little on the load as the gradient changes. As more of the train comes over the top her beat gets easier but she's still urging the train forward. Looking up we are passing the Long Mynd Hotel, a prominent landmark on the left hand side, with hotel guests watching us from the balconies and gardens and finally Church Stretton itself is in sight.

Chapter 14
Dropping like a stone

CHURCH STRETTON is a very pleasant small Shropshire town, made notable by the fact that if you are a fireman approaching from either direction, once you had passed through it, your troubles, for the time being at least were over. We're not booked to stop and its just as well for we are steadily accelerating as the rest of our train comes off the gradient. The distant and home signals are off and it's a clear run through. It's a slight downgrade from Little Stretton to Church Stretton and speed has rapidly risen, with the water level down to just on half a glass. Pressure is holding steady at 215 as both injectors, including the driver's side one have been put on to get water in the boiler and cool her down. From getting every last pound of steam out of her a minute ago, we now want to let her cool as we wont need much on a fast descent to Shrewsbury, so Stan keeps the regulator wide open and starts to wind the reverser back a notch at a time. Bursting out under the overbridge, past the box and onto the downgrade, 4037 leans to the curve and is starting to fly. Fred tells me that this is where we make up some time, as they will run as speedily as conditions and prudence allow to hand the train over to the LM Region at Shrewsbury 'right time'.

Coming up the hill on the other track is a British Railways Standard 5, 73094 that appears to be making heavy weather of a long string of banana vans bound from Crewe to Barry Dock. The vans are strung out along the flanks of a super-elevated S bend which would explain the difficulty, as being short wheelbase vans leaning their weight on the outside of two sharp curves at once, the effort to keep them moving smartly along would be considerable. The '5' is bubbling away at the safety valves, despite the huge effort and the towering grey tinged exhaust, so the job must be well in hand, but Fred tells me that the banana trains are a difficult proposition. These are empties on their way to Barry Dock for loading, and taking the empties down is bad enough but when they leave Barry docks loaded they run as fast perishable freight trains at express speed, and with the steam heat full on to ripen the bananas while in transit. The BR 5's don't have vacuum pumps, they have small ejectors to overcome any vacuum leakage, and in a train of vans like this there are a large number of potential leaks. This gives a demand for steam big enough to daunt the most proficient fireman and is like running a heavy passenger train in the middle of winter. 'You'd be surprised how heavy a trainload of hanging bananas are' he said sagely, pipe in hand.

A train of 40-50 vans has a far greater rolling resistance than a passenger train of similar weight, and even though many of these vans have roller bearings the sheer work of running them and heating them at the same time makes their efficient working a job for experts, handling locos in excellent order. 73094 is regarded as one of Shrewsbury's best 5MT's, and from its clean lined-green livery appears to be not long out of the works. He tells me the engine will work through to Barry but the crew should change at either Hereford or Pontypool Road. However, given the summertime shortage of crews he wouldn't be surprised if they worked right through to Barry, as he did himself on one of these trains a month previously. There's usually no hanging about as these trains are coded as fast perishable freight and have the priority of express passenger trains. 'They won't be doing much frying up on that job', he said 'they'll be lucky to swallow a cup of tea'.

The track is curving away in front of us on a downgrade of about 1 in 100 , and Stan just wants to let her run in front of the train under drifting steam, which is enough to cushion everything nicely and keep the front end hot and well lubricated. He's wound her back to about 15% cut-off with a full open regulator and she's chattering nicely. The firedoors are open and the flap down and Fred shuts the dampers to try to cool her. There will be no more firing now – he can sit down and look for signals. Stan need only check the train slightly with the brake now and again through the curves and to keep her running between 60 and 80 on the downhill stretches. He quickly shuts off the driver's-side injector as water level is now at two-thirds of a glass and this with the engine pointing downhill. They leave the exhaust injector on fine feed as she is still using some steam, and this should hold water level steady until they hit the flat again near Coleham depot. Fred's watch tells us that we are only a minute adrift by his reckoning so fast steady running with no nasty surprises will be the order of the day.

Approaching Leebotwood on a 1 in 100 down we pass a Shrewsbury 'Castle' no. 5095 'Barbury Castle' coming unassisted up the hill in fine style with 12 coaches. She's a double-chimney 'Castle', and Fred tells me that they are freer running than the single stack ones like ours, with a higher superheat boiler and mechanical lubrication to the front end. He rathers the older version himself, but he does say that the double stack 'Castles' seem to manage better with indifferent coal, which gives more of a margin for error when circumstances are going the wrong way. He says we were fortunate with our engine and the high importance Shrewsbury and Newton Abbot attach to engines on double home turns. The best engines with the best coal are put on these jobs, and 4037 is in very good condition. If, by dint of circumstance they had been given a higher mileage 'Castle', longer out of the shops, with a tender of doubtful coal then they would have struggled to Bristol with thirteen on and probably dropped time, and refused to take the fourteenth coach at Temple Meads as that would have stymied them completely. It was only because they had complete confidence in 4037 that they were agreeable to the overload, because they both knew that a good engine with good coal would do it quite competently. It wouldn't be easy, but at least there would be no excuses and form filling at the end of it. The '5' and her banana vans will have to run smartly to keep out of the way of 5095 following a few blocks behind, but Fred reckons that the banana train once over Stretton summit will run very smartly downhill all the way to either Ludlow or Woofferton before being looped to let 5095 by. It all depends on how the 5's crew decides to run her and whether they get a clear road.

Leebotwood's signals are clear and with a wave from the box we pour through at a steady 75. Stan's giving her a touch of brake here and there to steady the train on the straights so that it runs easily through the curves. 4037 is running quietly with a breath of steam keeping everything turning over and herself slightly ahead of the train. She's heeling left and right to the super-elevation of the curves, with no jarring or vibration and riding over pointwork like a Rolls-Royce. The train is clattering smoothly behind, still with all windows open, and apart from a slight brake application from time to time we run smoothly on downhill towards Dorrington.

There's a freight in the loop at Dorrington, awaiting our passage. A long train of vans headed by an LMR 8F. We roar by, with the sound of our passing reflected off the vans and passing us southbound is No. 6000 'King George V' himself, complete with burnished brass bell at the head of thirteen coaches, some of which are Royal Mail vans. The 'mail for Penzance' Fred tells me, which 6000 will take to Bristol, or even Plymouth, but this crew will only take 6000 to Pontypool Road at most, unless circumstances dictate some overtime in which case they may go on to Bristol. He had worked that train a fortnight previously and had ended up going to Hereford, Pontypool and Severn Tunnel Junction on successive days before being relieved such is the pressure on crewing in the summer months. There is plenty of southbound perishable freight and passenger traffic, so no wonder we saw a queue of freights at Hereford.

Just past Dorrington is a short stretch of uphill running to Condover, but with 4037 and her train running at 75, the uphill only serves to slow us down slightly to just under 60 and we run steadily through Condover, whistling to warn two platelayers near the box. The valley is opening out now and Shrewsbury is in sight. Just in front of us is a large stone crushing plant at Bayston Hill with a train of ballast wagons being loaded and a clean BR Standard tank 82003 standing nearby waiting to take them away. It's a long left hand curve through Bayston Hill followed by a right hand and then the long straight into Shrewsbury. This is where the serious braking will be done once all of the train is on the straight and as soon as we are off the curves Stan takes ten inches of vacuum out of the system and immediately we feel the whole train steady and start to gently slow. The crosshead vacuum pump on the 'Castle' will take some of the sting out of it but this brings speed down to a steady and manageable 55 and just up ahead on the straight we can see the distant and outer home signals for Shrewsbury Sutton Bridge Junction showing clear, but another application will take us smoothly through there at 45 or even just below. This will allow us to run through the curves past Coleham depot and into Shrewsbury, but at a speed that can be easily killed if we come upon a home signal that is late in clearing due to a conflicting movement up ahead.

The section from Sutton Bridge into Shrewsbury is quite busy, due to traffic to the Severn Valley and Cambrian lines as well as the light engines from Coleham to Shrewsbury station, so our crew are expecting to be checked at some point and keeping the running of the train strictly in hand is careful cautious enginemanship. A sharp stop can throw passengers off their feet and bring luggage down off racks onto heads and as Fred says' 'We don't want any slip-ups this close to the shed or the finish', and so 4037 runs quietly through the outer Shrewsbury suburbs, past Sutton Bridge sidings and clattering over the junction we pass Coleham depot on the right hand side and curve round to the left towards Abbey Foregate and Severn Bridge Junction. Coleham depot is full of locomotives being serviced, and used to be a joint GWR and LMS depot until Nationalisation, and it still has separate allocations of both types of engines even now, with a leavening of BR Standard machines to ring the changes. Fred tells me that its an interesting depot as with six routes out of Shrewsbury, and with its variety of visiting motive power footplate crews get experience of types of work here that it would take them many years to gain elsewhere.

There's a short stretch here over a viaduct that takes us over the rooftops past Abbey Foregate signalbox and finally the huge Severn Bridge Junction box comes into view. This colossal mechanical box controls all movement at the south end of Shrewsbury including the triangular junction giving access to three routes. Its about 50 feet high and must be 150 feet long by about 20 feet wide, and needs three signalmen and two booking boys to run it. We're signalled to run in to the centre island platform for an engine change and handover to the Midland Region and from Fred's watch we are slightly before time, so the final plummet from Church Stretton finally set the books straight. There's plenty going on here, a freshly overhauled 46170 'British Legion' is backing round one leg of the triangle during a turning move to get it pointing the right way for Crewe and over in the bay are two 'Castles' 4099 'Kilgerran Castle' and 5023 'Brecon Castle' awaiting trains for the south which they are to take over from Midland engines. Just on the other side of the box is 7025 'Sudeley Castle' all shone up and carrying a 'Cambrian Coast Express' headboard, ready to take over from an Aberystwyth-based 'Manor' for the next leg of the train's run to London Paddington.

Picking our way cautiously through all of this we roll round the bend and into the long island platform, running in to pass 46255 'City of Hereford' standing on the centre road waiting to change over. This engine is obviously ex-works, by its appearance and is being used on the Crewe-Shrewsbury relief turns to fill in between overnight jobs on the Perth sleepers from Crewe. Stan tells me he's been to Crewe and back a few times on these while at Shrewsbury, and they are a lot bigger than a 'Castle' in many ways. Their fireboxes have to be well filled to get them to do anything, but once they are properly prepared, there isn't a train they can't handle. He reckons this fourteen coach deadweight we have dragged up from Newton will be worked smartly away by this engine which will laugh at the load figuratively speaking and probably be blowing off all the way to Crewe. An LMR driver told him that they were designed to work sixteen coach trains all the way from London to Glasgow in six hours, which is some going for trains of that size and weight, and they do work like that on overnight sleeper trains regularly. They are just starting to be replaced by diesels on this sort of work which is why we now see them on these filling in jobs to keep their utilisation high. The men who work them hold them in very high regard, and know that whatever the load and conditions, if they do the job properly, they will want for neither steam nor power. The driver and fireman are looking out for us as we run past. The driver is a very old salt and the fireman looks about fifteen. Fred makes a comment as we roll by and the driver starts laughing and nods at his fireman who is standing in the cab entrance. Fred tells me the driver is one of 'Crewe depot's elder statesmen' and is very close to retirement. The fireman is probably a willing conscript off a Crewe shunting tank who has swapped an afternoon in Basford Hall yards for a run to Shrewsbury and back on a thoroughbred Stanier Pacific.

He tells me that the Shrewsbury relief turn for the cross-country expresses like this is used to 'run-in' locomotives just out of works after overhaul, and the older drivers near retirement or on light duty are put on it along with young firemen. This neatly kills three birds with one stone. The old boys get 'new' engines and an early finish, the works get the engines run in by experts and the youngsters get a taste of express working under the tutelage of old hands where they can run fast enough to get the taste but not for long enough to get into serious trouble if they get the firing wrong.

They have just taken water and are waiting for us to get clear so they can take over. We roll gently to a stand and as we do Stan winds her swiftly into reverse gear and lets 4037 lean back against the train. There's a loud thud from the rear of the tender and in a few moments the passenger shunter appears waving us away. Looking out for clear signals, Stan opens the regulator and we move smartly away and across the crossovers at the north end of Shrewsbury station. Released from the weight of the train 4037 is like a different engine, and Stan lets her roll forward until clear of the points. A quick code on the whistle and the north end signalman changes the points behind us to allow us a clear run back through Shrewsbury station heading for the depot. 46255 is moving gently forward on the adjacent track as we run back and in less than a minute she will be coupled on to our train by the shunter in heavy gauntlets who is waiting by the first coach.

We are moving gently back down the other side of the island platform that we ran in on. The platform is full of a summer crowd with cases and children in tow and as we move towards the far end the signal giving access to the triangle and Coleham depot is against us and Stan lets 4037 slide smoothly to a stand to await the road. A man in an open necked shirt, standing smoking by an open door of our train, stubs his cigarette and walks over to us. 'Did you lads bring in this train', he asks, jerking his thumb back over his shoulder. When Fred nodded he said ' Damn fine work, I've been watching and listening all the way up. I'm a driver at Carlisle and we wouldn't have worked one of these like that', nodding at 4037' we'd have worked it a good deal lighter and taken our time with this load, but all the same it was nice to see.'

Fred and Stan looked mildly surprised, and thanked him. Our admirer had to go as whistles were blowing on the other side and as he turns to rejoin his train, our signal clears and we move sharply out over the junction and past Severn Bridge signalbox onto the Hereford line for the short run, tender first to Coleham depot. A 'Manor' class engine, 7812 'Erlestoke Manor' in sparkling condition coasts past us, running into Shrewsbury at the head of the ten chocolate and cream coaches of the 'Cambrian Coast Express' from Pwllheli and Aberystwyth bound for Paddington, and as we run further out two locomotives coupled together, 73129 a BR 'Caprotti' Class 5 and 5967 'Bickmarsh Hall' pass us creeping in to the station one block behind the 'Manor' and it's train, being sent down to work later trains. The line is running out on a viaduct over Shrewsbury's rooftops and as we pass Abbey Foregate signalbox the signals and road are set to take us onto the depot. Stan shuts off and lets 4037 coast gently into the shed entrance road and bringing speed right down to walking pace we pick our way across the shed roads to the ashpit where we stop just short of 7015 'Carn Brea Castle' which brought in the main portion of our train twenty minutes earlier. We were the relief and we were packed to the doors so what was their trip like? The shedmen are at work clearing the fire on 7015, and just beyond a Cardiff 'Britannia', 70024 is having its ashpan dumped into the pits. There are engines of all types standing around here, as Shrewsbury was a joint GWR/LMS shed and the variety of machinery is immense at this inter-regional meeting point. Another 'Castle', 5059 'Earl St.Aldwyn' is standing on the exit road ready to run to the station tender first, to be followed by an LMR 'Jubilee' 45590 'Travancore'. Fred tells me he quite often works 'Jubilee's and 'Royal Scots' down to Pontypool on relief trains and as a GW man he quite likes them, 'once you get used to their little ways' as they have better cabs than Western engines. On some occasions he has worked them to Cardiff, but that is comparatively rare as the diagrams say they have to come off at Pontypool Road. Both of them like the LMR 'Royal Scots' with the double stack, which they say are a good coach better on Llanvihangel bank than a 'Castle' and a far more powerful engine than their compact size suggests. Fred and Stan are preparing to leave. Fred pulls out of the locker a beautiful brassbound mahogany dome top box that looks like a miniature steamer trunk. This is an engineman's box, which contains small tools, spare gauge glasses, working time tables, and drivers tickets as well as his private supply of tea and sugar.His other gear is in an old army holdall. Stan seems to have everything packed into a large leather guard's satchel and my own holdall is retrieved from its hiding place.

The toolboxes are locked with two padlocks and the keys are to be handed in when booking off. They are each attached to a length of chain which has a large washer stamped '4037' attached to it. There is little chance of walking off absent-mindedly with these. This saves much to-ing and fro-ing to the stores when preparing engines as only consumable stores such as oil, corks or trimmings should need to be booked out – at least that's the theory. The oil feeders, the cylinder oil jack and the flag and detonators in their sealed tinplate canister are put in the footplate bucket with the handbrush, and after a quick look round that all is secure – regulator shut, cylinder cocks open, engine in mid-gear and tender handbrake firmly on it's time to go.

There's 1500 gallons in the tank and the coal is still within a shovel's length of reach in the tender. The fire has subsided to a bright orange, and can either be rebuilt or easily thrown out depending on what 4037 does next and how soon. Two shedmen arrive off 7015 and set about disposing 4037. There's smokebox, ashpan and fire-cleaning to be done and they know our crew so the 'crack' flows thick and fast. An examining fitter arrives and Fred and Stan tell him that 4037 appears 'in good nick'. He nods and continues in his examination anyway. Fred will fill in a repair card in the lobby, so there is very little chance of anything being missed and 4037 should be in good order for her next trip, probably back to Newton Abbot. Climbing down is like getting back to dry land after a spell afloat. My legs are a bit shaky and I have to lean against the tender footstep for support and to get my bearings. My holdall is passed down and Frank Lewis and the crew step down and head for the lobby to sign off. I follow, a little unsteadily at first, hot, sticky, dusty, tired and more than ready for a few pints of beer and a bath, probably in that order.

Chapter 15
Tail Lamp

I HAD been fortunate to see an expert display of enginemanship, under very good conditions of weather, load, and road. Frank Lewis pointed out that what I had seen was about as good as it gets under current conditions, and he regarded them as a highly expert crew. The problem the railways now had was that men were leaving for cleaner jobs with regular hours, often under family pressure and it was becoming a lot harder to maintain schedules and timings as many depots were undermanned especially those near industrial areas. Stan had been borrowed from Pontypool Road to help Shrewsbury out, and they were lucky to have him in Frank Lewis's view. Fred was in the Shrewsbury top link and regularly ran to Newton Abbot and back over two days, so on a job like that you needed a mate who really knew what he was doing. The whole reliability of the express train service in those days was down to such human factors. Here we were, on the cusp of the space age, and the running of express trains was governed by the ability of a man to swing a shovelfull of coal, albeit that the quality of the coal being shovelled was variable depending on which part of the country you were in and where the coal came from. Add to this that the last steam locomotive had been built the previous year, and diesels were becoming more prevalent and the writing was on the wall.

Dieselisation would take the human factor and the high degree of skill involved in working steam, right out of the business of train running. It would be several years yet but it would be the end of an era. It had already happened in the United States and Canada and it would happen here too. In Frank Lewis's day, and possibly Fred's too, a footplate job was highly prized for the continuity it offered and the working conditions were no worse than other industrial jobs and in some cases a lot better. In Fred's case he had joined during the Depression years, and was glad to have a job, but Stan had joined post-War when matters were starting to change. All three had had some family connection with the railway, which no doubt got them a start and all three had commented on how the post war industrial expansion and improvements in working conditions had impacted the quality and supply of young men willing to put up with such conditions of work. They all felt they were too far in to get out now, but interestingly all of them foresaw a much slimmed down railway with less men and equipment, and hence less chance of advancement. Working conditions on diesels would be better, they had seen enough to know that, but they all said that the sheer concentration and level of skill required was less and it was a lot less hard work. I had seen enough hard work today under nearly ideal conditions. I shuddered to think what it was like to work a heavy express or freight over the same road on a black, cold winters night with bad coal, a loco not in the best condition, an inexperienced fireman, and try and keep time - but it was being done day after day, until the diesels finally come. A diesel cab has a level of convenience and comfort found in a motor car and that is the standard that is now required, and as they become more numerous so the old skills and their fine nuances will be lost in the mists of time. I hope that this will help to preserve that and encourage others to dig that little bit deeper in their pursuit of what was, and is, man's *friendliest* invention - the steam locomotive.

J.B 31st July 1961

Author's Note - March 2006: Substantially as written at the time. Main line locomotive preservation didn't start until two years later when Alan Pegler bought 60103 'Flying Scotsman'. There were about twenty locomotives scheduled for official preservation, and 4073 'Caerphilly Castle' had been moved to the Science Museum in South Kensington the previous year. We thought that steam would disappear entirely, and very little would be left for future generations to pore over. We certainly didn't imagine that the main line steam locomotive would return, as it has to the tune of nearly 1000 preserved locomotives in Britain and many of those under active restoration or in full working order. All of this was done by private groups and individuals who provided both the labour and finance to realise it. One other individual played a huge part. The late Dai Woodham, a scrap metal merchant of Barry Dock, who although a shrewd businessman, held off putting over 300 steam locomotives to the torch until ways and means could be found to secure them for preservation and reuse. When the definitive history of the Age(s) of Steam is written, for the Second Coming is not yet over, the legend of Woodham's Yard will feature highly as without him, the miracle of main line locomotive preservation and running would not have occurred.

Very little, if any State sponsorship has assisted in the preservation of steam locomotives in Britain. Contrast this with the vast sums poured into 'culture and the arts', yet Britain was both the crucible and birthplace of railways, and for many years Britain's railways were among the world's finest. Now the official and acceptable line appears to be to denigrate and despise them at every turn, and overlook the vast, wasted national asset in our midst. Looking at Switzerland and France one can readily see the sort of unrealised potential that exists. We appear to lack the willpower and expertise to make the sustained effort to put it right as it is far too easy and convenient to use motor transport, and railways aren't deemed a vote winner. Until of course, 2010 when the oil starts to run out......

James Barry
March 2006

Two shots of 4037, beautifully lit, standing at Exeter
23rd June 1962 - two months before withdrawl.
Total mileage run: 2,429,722 since December 1910
Photos : R.C.Riley/Transport Treasury

This was exactly as I remember her - I first saw these pictures
45 years after my journey. In a larger size you can almost step in
and walk around.....long gone but never forgotten.

Climbing Filton Bank at Narroways Hill (burnt smokebox,
leaking glands but a blossom at the safety valves) c.1955
Photo: George F. Heiron

Royal Oak 9th September 1961
Photo: R.C.Riley

With a 'boy's train' - Stoke Canon 18th July 1959
Photo R.C.Riley/Transport Treasury

At Swindon with the 'Merchant Venturer' - 17th September 1952.
Photo: M.Robertson/Transport Treasury

4037 running alongside the Teign estuary near Newton Abbot
during the glorious summer of 1959 - 17 July 1959.
Photo R.C. Riley/Transport Treasury

Slightly earlier - Whiteball summit - 27th June 1953
Photo: A.Carway/Transport Treasury

4037 stands at Penzance (83G) - 6th September 1956
Photo: Eric Sawford

4037 stands at Plymouth Laira depot, 30th August 1961 –
this was the view I got of her as we walked down off
the platform ramp at Temple Meads to board.
Photo: R.C Riley/Transport Treasury

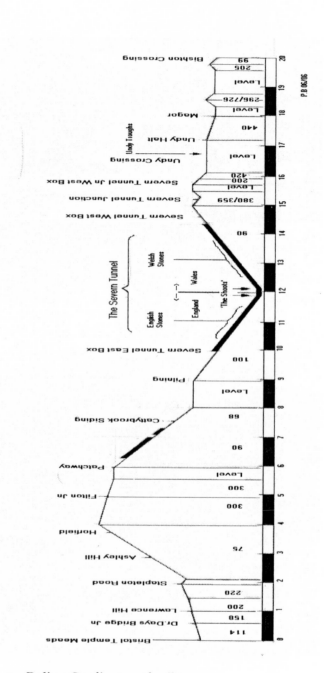

Diagram 1.
Bristol Temple Meads to Bishton Crossing

1 - Ruling Gradients and mileage -
Bristol Temple Meads to Bishton Crossing

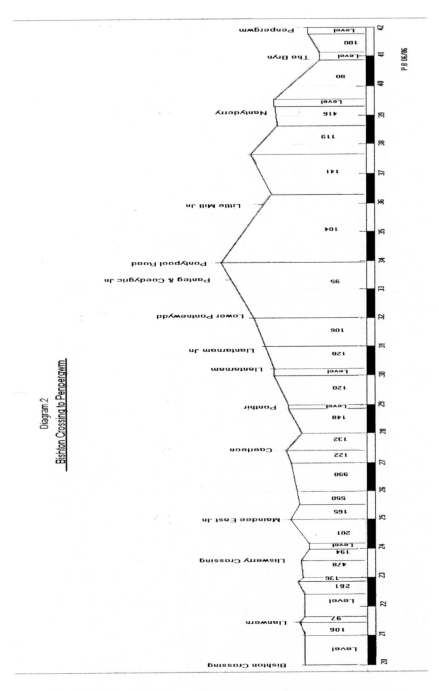

Diagram 2
Bishton Crossing to Penpergwm

Gradients and Route - Bishton Crossing to Penpergwm

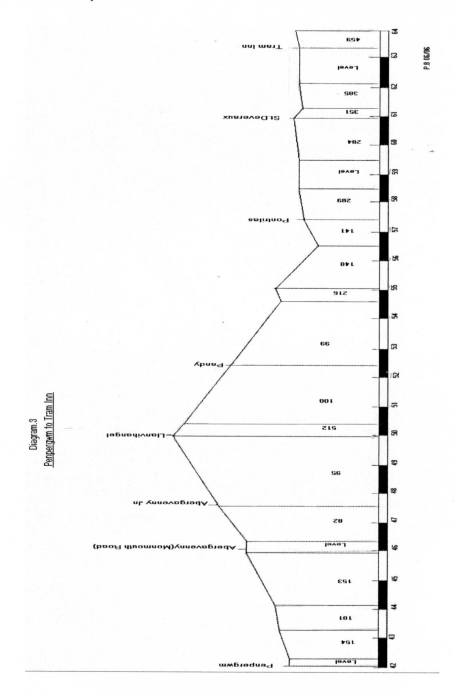

Gradient 3 - Penpergwm to Tram Inn

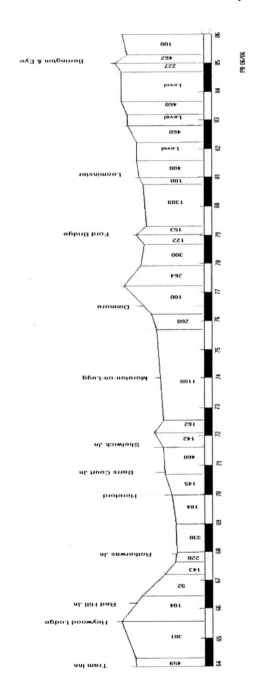

Diagram 4

Tram Inn to Berrington & Eye

Gradient 4 - Tram Inn to Berrington & Eye

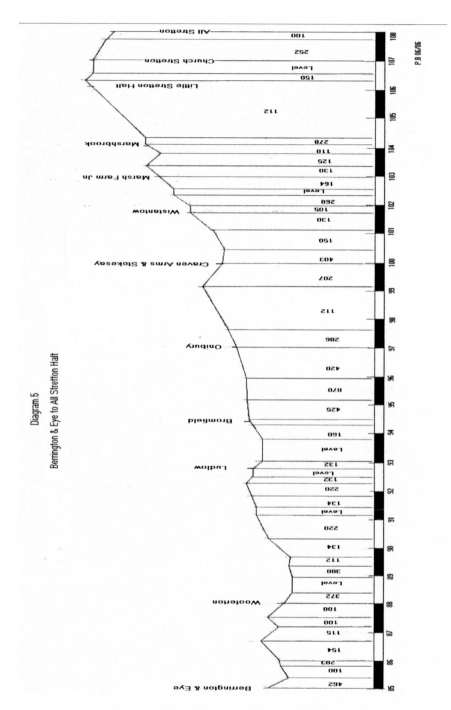

Diagram 5
Berrington & Eye to All Stretton Halt

P.B 06/06

Gradient 5 - Berrington & Eye to All Stretton

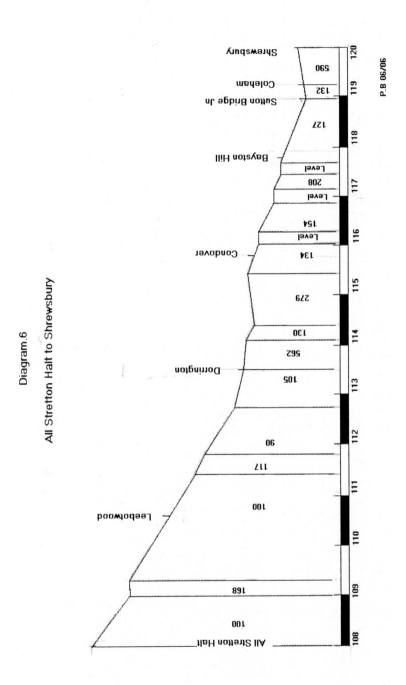

Diagram.6

All Stretton Halt to Shrewsbury

Gradient 6 - All Stretton to Shrewsbury

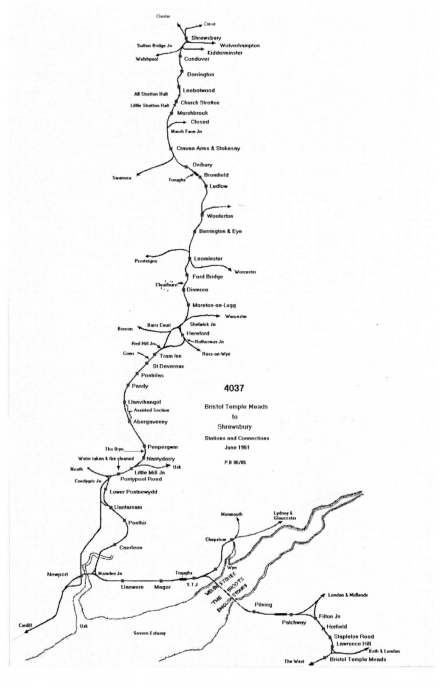

Map of route showing major stations and connections

Printed in the United Kingdom
by Lightning Source UK Ltd.
115204UKS00001B/514-519